THE
CLOUDS
YE
SO MUCH
DREAD

THE CLOUDS YE SO MUCH DREAD

HARD TIMES AND THE KINDNESS OF GOD

Hannah K. Grieser

canonpress
Moscow, Idaho

Published by Canon Press

P.O. Box 8729, Moscow, Idaho 83843

800.488.2034 | www.canonpress.com

Hannah K. Grieser, *The Clouds Ye So Much Dread: Hard Times and the Kindness of God*

Copyright ©2017 by Hannah K. Grieser

Cover design by James Engerbretson
Interior design by Valerie Anne Bost

Printed in the United States of America.

Library of Congress Cataloging-in-Publication Data is forthcoming.

18 19 20 21 22 23 24   9 8 7 6 5 4 3 2

For my mother, a true daughter of Sarah

Table of Contents

Foreword

by
N.D. Wilson

Hannah Grieser (formerly Atwood) is one of those people whom I feel as if I have always known. There are a few of those folks around in this small town where we both grew up. In Hannah's case, I don't remember when I met her, but I know it was in elementary school. In 1996, we graduated from Logos School together in a class of only seventeen students. (Classes that size get to know each other pretty well.) After college and graduate school, I worked under her father at New Saint Andrews College. Later, I co-taught college freshmen alongside her husband. Rory, my eldest son, entered kindergarten with Jonah, Hannah's eldest. For years, our families lived one block apart on the same street, and I have many memories of our sons' lively conversations in the backseat during carpool. I watched them together in school plays, in spelling bees and speech meets, on baseball diamonds and basketball courts. As I write this, I am keeping one eye on the clock, knowing that I will soon jump in my truck and drive to watch the first basketball game of our boys' sophomore season.

Many of the memories I have of our long cohabitation of this small town have gone murky, but one Saturday stands out perfectly clearly. Our sons were playing in a summer lacrosse league together, and the day was perfect; flocks of brightly lit clouds were migrating through our vast Idaho sky, above our small, battling offspring. I was standing on the sideline with Hannah's husband, talking about nothing important. While it must have been warm, hot even, I only remember a cold and certain knowledge of wrongness creeping up inside me. Rory, always a mulish defender, was himself. But Jonah, normally quick and slippery on attack, a certainty to score, indefatigable, was not himself at all. He looked exhausted, beaten, even limp. I asked his father what was wrong. He told me that it might be mono. But I had seen mono before, and Jonah's transformation struck me as far more extreme. Not too long after that Saturday, we heard the terrifying news. Jonah had been diagnosed with leukemia.

And this leads me back to Hannah, back to my memories, and then to this book you hold in your hands. The Hannah I knew in school was smart, tough, artistic, dry, independent, unemotional, and competitive in a way that never showed her effort. I never would have used any adjectives connected to fear to describe her. She was never timid, never a complainer, never one to bemoan an obstacle. Imagine being a young girl and being pulled out of your (very close) class to go live in Kenya. Or Poland. But she never showed any sign of upheaval, no sign of nervousness beforehand. And upon her return, she shrugged off her adventurous exiles like they were nothing. She simply reentered our class. She didn't show any worry about how much she had missed, about how much living her friends had done without her (or any new friends she had left behind). Hannah never showed any fearfulness at all during our school years (at least not to the boys). In adulthood, even as a mother to a son with leukemia, she also never wore her fear on the outside. It was there, she acknowledged it, but she never made it her brand, or even an accessory.

Now that I have this book in my hands, I feel like I never knew her at all. Hannah writing about fear? Hannah struggling with fear? This journey she has gone on, this path she has walked, has changed her. How could it not? She is still an artist. She is still smart, dry, and independent. But she is no longer trying to hide her effort.

This is not a thing that could be shrugged off. What she faced, externally and internally, is now painted in this book, in print, for everyone to see. She has taken her trials and the trials of her family, and she has set out to distill their value for the sake of others. She may have bottled up her struggles, but those bottles are now meant to be exported and opened. Through all of this, she has distilled a vintage of God's grace that is lovely and encouraging, potent and tender. On these pages, she offers comfort, companionship, and guidance for anyone facing any kind of fear, which is to say, for mortals, for all of us. And I, for one, am grateful.

N.D. WILSON
December 2017

Preface

This book is not a theological treatise. This book is not a memoir. This book is not exactly a collection of essays, either. This book, I suppose, falls somewhere into the cracks in between.

It's true that this book is about me. (It's hard to avoid that when writing stories from my own life.) But this is also a book about trials big and small—about cancer, about suffering, about death—and especially about the temptation to fear. Sounds like a real downer, I know. But let me assure you that, while these frightful things are the *reason* for this book, none of them is the *point* of this book. The real point is God Himself and the comfort that His fearful and afflicted children can find only by trusting Him.

However, while attempting to write the pages that follow, I didn't begin with a clear point in mind. I started by simply going through tidbits I'd already written—blog posts, journal entries, notes jotted on the backs of receipts, looking for ideas and recollections, or even turns of phrase that struck me as significant. At first, I rolled along down the well-worn ruts of memory lane, pausing at a familiar landmark here, enjoying a favorite view there. But eventually, I found myself steering toward old byways that I hadn't especially wanted to revisit and turning over long-forgotten stones where I rediscovered some darker bits that I had hoped never to unearth. A lot of disparate memories surfaced, and none of them seemed to have anything, other than *me*, in common. This turns out to be a rather weak premise for a book: a few memories about cancer and world travel, plus some anecdotes about health fads and a handful of miscellaneous thoughts on money and childbirth. No unifying principle. No theme. I couldn't even pitch that book idea to *myself*.

However, I wanted to write, and I had agreed to write, so write I did, praying that I could find a thread that would tie this whole scattered hodge-podge together.

Then, early this year, I was asked to join a small panel discussion at the local Christian college on the topic of feminine strength, which is not a subject to which I'd really given much thought. What *does* it mean to be a "strong Christian woman"? Later that week, as I was reading 1 Peter 3:6, the description of Sarah jumped out at me: "Sarah obeyed Abraham, calling him lord. And you are her children, if you do good and do not fear anything that is frightening." So often, the focus—and the attendant controversy over submission—centers on the first half of that verse, while the second half gets lost in the skirmish. But as I read, it was the second half that stood out: "You are her children, if you do good and do not fear anything that is frightening."

Do not fear anything that is frightening. This assumes that some things we face *are* frightening, including, one would think, being married to a man like Abraham. (How massively would *you* have freaked out when word of that whole sacrifice-of-Isaac incident reached you?) So the apostle Peter holds up Sarah's fearlessness as something for us to aspire to—*#goals*, anyone? With the question of "What is a strong Christian woman?" in mind, I realized that fearlessness is one of the chief traits of all the great women in Scripture: Sarah following Abraham's call from God to pursue some seemingly crazy and dangerous endeavors, which required letting go of fear and instead trusting God's promises. Rahab hiding enemy spies because she had heard and believed in the power of the God of Israel. Deborah marching out with the armies of Israel—and their weak-kneed commander—against the iron chariots of Sisera. Jael, "most blessed of women,"[1] inviting the enemy king into her tent to pound a stake through his skull. Ruth, leaving everything she had known to follow Naomi and Naomi's God into a land where Moabites like her were despised. Abigail, both undercutting the tyrannical folly of her husband and confronting an armed and angry future king David at the same time. Esther, taking her life in her hands to approach the king with the words, "If I perish, I perish" on her lips. Mary, Jesus' mother, bravely and joyfully receiving the news of a pregnancy that could lead to public ridicule and to rejection by the man she planned to marry. And so many more.

These women had courage. They had *chutzpah.* They had guts. But more fundamentally, they had *faith*—faith in God, faith in His promises, faith in His goodness, faith in His justice, faith in His saving power. These women did "not fear anything that is frightening." Fear[2] would mean hearing God's promises and then calling Him a liar. Fighting fear and learning to trust God is, for me, a constant struggle. But these women were strong because they

---

1 Judges 5:24, from Deborah's song of praise after the defeat of Sisera's army—a phrase that almost exactly mirrors the words of Elizabeth to Mary in Luke 1:42: "Blessed are you among women!" Jael and Mary are both called blessed by these mothers in Israel, and both used powerfully by God to crush the head of the serpent.

2 By which I mean fear of that which is *not* God.

fearlessly believed God, and we are Sarah's daughters if we do the same.

As I meditated on this, it struck me that one of the themes that ran through everything I'd already been writing was the tug-o-war between fear and faith, between dread of life's storm clouds and trust in the One who holds us fast. The more I wrote, the more clear it became that, regardless of the incident I was recalling, my fears and God's faithfulness were the common threads that tie these pages together and form the heart of this book.

So this book is, in one sense, an autobiography; I tell it in the first person simply because I lived it in the first person. Plenty of memoirs and biographies out there can inspire (or horrify) you with their tales of unparalleled tragedy and triumph. This is not that book. My life really hasn't been anything very exceptional. My goal is not, primarily, to tell you who I am. Rather, through stories of common, run-of-the-mill fears—fears like yours and mine—my goal is to show you, in some small way, who *God* is. He is extraordinary. He is faithful. We can trust Him with our very lives. So we need not be afraid of anything that is frightening.

CHAPTER 1

A Spirit
Not of Fear

Truly, truly, I say to you, unless a grain of wheat falls into the earth and dies, it remains alone; but if it dies, it bears much fruit (John 12:24).

Age twenty-two was, if not the best of times, at least the most optimistic. My college diploma had scarcely begun to collect dust, my job as a graphic designer at a magazine was filling my nine-to-fives (and then some) with just the kind of duties I had planned toward for four years, and I had recently celebrated my first wedding anniversary to a handsome, hard-working man who was beginning his senior year of college and already sending out job applications in anticipation of a career as a teacher.

My husband, Jayson, and I lived on a quiet street in a sunny little basement apartment filled with shiny new wedding gifts. We enjoyed a lovely little circle of friends. We attended a thriving church. We watched our modest savings grow, little by little, each month. We even had a retirement account, for pity's sake. And, looking ahead, I envisioned an unbroken succession of picture-perfect years stretching before us like a lush expanse of suburban lawn. At twenty-two, my life—and the life I imagined—were as sweet, as simple, and, in some respects, as substantial, as a cloud of cotton candy.

Then, one day in September, I learned that I was pregnant. And suddenly my spun-sugar prospects seemed to dissolve.

This pregnancy had not been unexpected; we had planned for this. We had prayed for this. We had wanted this. And, although I'd been apprehensive, I assumed that when the day came, I'd be ready to face it with courage, dignity, and grace. But when the reality of the news finally sank in, I stared into the bathroom mirror, gripping the edge of the counter, and could feel only one sensation: terror.

As soon as those two little lines showed up on the pregnancy test, Fear came knocking, and I foolishly flung wide the doors of my heart and invited her in. I'd met her before, on many occasions, and she had sometimes visited for a day or two—maybe even for a couple of weeks—as an uninvited guest before I sent her packing. But this time, Fear had arrived with a moving van and had quickly filled and redecorated every corner with her collection of sharp objects and heavy furnishings. In the process, she had unceremoniously torn down most of the light fixtures, shuttered the windows, tossed my faithful friend Joy onto the curb with the trash, and settled in for an extended stay.

Long before Fear's official move-in date, I'd already anticipated the huge adjustments that would be in store for me as a mother. Before the arrival of my first child, I had struggled at times with worries about almost everything to do with motherhood—the nursing, the diaper changing, the lack of sleep, the social adjustments, the decisions about education, the discipline, and so on. I had invested very little of my imaginative resources on the joys of motherhood and the blessings children could bring. I don't remember playing much with baby dolls as a child. I played doctor. I played store proprietor. I played orphan. I played Lego architect. But I don't remember my childhood aspirations inclining toward playing the role of "mommy." As I got older, young children often struck me as more of a bother than a blessing, and as a high schooler, after a particularly horrid babysitting episode, I had gone so far as to announce that I never wanted to have children. At the time, I absolutely meant it.

Later, when I started college, I remember taking one of those personality tests to help determine a course of studies best suited to my natural gifts, and do you know what career type I scored lowest on? Caregiver. My "natural gifts" were, apparently, *least* suited toward taking care of the weak and helpless. And if that's not a perfect description of what a young mother (and, let's be honest, every Christian) must do, I don't know what is.

This is one of the reasons I bristle a bit when Christians talk about our "callings" as if they were nothing more than the career choices that correspond with our natural talents and desires. In order for someone to be called, someone else must be doing the calling. And that Someone calls us to love our crooked neighbors and to bless those who hate us and to lay our lives down—regardless of whether we would be more naturally inclined to do precisely the opposite. In fact, none of us is naturally gifted at these things; we must be *super*naturally gifted. When we are called, it is sometimes to do the very things that most clearly expose to us how inadequate we are in our own strength and how much we need the Spirit of Christ to fill and equip us to do the hard things that He requires of us. For me, one of those hard things was learning to be a mother.

This new role was going to be the biggest stretch—emotionally, spiritually, and physically—of any I'd yet experienced. I was in for a challenge. That much I knew. I had no delusions about what creature comforts, what social connections, and what career opportunities I'd likely be setting aside when I became a mother, and it frightened me. I was, in short, afraid to lose my life as I had known it. But even these concerns paled in comparison to my fear of just one solitary thing: giving birth.

I was aware that this wasn't an entirely rational fear. I knew that, while childbirth throughout much of the world—and through most of history—was fraught with deadly dangers, childbirth in a twenty-first century American hospital was overwhelmingly likely to result in both a healthy mother and child. My own mother had experienced two very uneventful pregnancies and two healthy births, and so had most of my aunts and cousins. We come from "good breeding stock," as one of my aunts once put it. So it wasn't that I believed I was destined for a tragic birth story. If pressed, I could have rattled off any number of reasons to look forward to a safe, uncomplicated "birth experience." But as my due date drew nearer, I just couldn't shake the sense of impending doom.

MY HUSBAND AND I DUTIFULLY ATTENDED A childbirth class at the local hospital, filling out our worksheets, reading the recommended books, and raising our hands to answer questions. If I had been asked to take a quiz about the step-by-step progression of labor and delivery, I don't doubt that I could have aced it. I studied so much, I could probably have written a textbook-ready essay, with scientific accuracy, on the distinct stages of childbirth and the various comfort measures that would ease the process. I was one hundred percent academically ready to give birth.

However, when it came to facing the real-life challenge I'd so diligently studied, head knowledge seemed worse than useless: the more I learned about what was coming, the more I feared it. I had been around plenty of sweet, joyful young mothers, but even that turned out to be less than encouraging since it was some of those same ladies who had unwittingly helped to plant the seeds of fear in the rich soil of my imagination in the first place. What is it about proximity to infants that gives women an almost irresistible desire to share the worst possible birth stories in a sort of sick parlor game of one-upmanship? "Oh yeah? That's pretty awful. But, let me tell you about the time my sister hemorrhaged so badly she *almost died!*" Over the years, I had listened at baby showers to so many older women share tales of horrifying, blood-and-guts exploits in the delivery room that my mental picture of childbirth had gradually come to resemble the opening scenes from *Saving Private Ryan*.

One evening, about halfway through my pregnancy, when our birth class gathered to watch a video depicting several different women in the throes of labor, I very nearly fainted. And I am not one who faints. I can laugh about it now, but I literally had to close my eyes, drop my head toward my knees, and take deep breaths to keep from passing out during the video, filled as it was with moaning women, shouts of pain, and infants covered in blood and slime. It was ghastly. I could not tell whether the spasms I was feeling in my belly were my baby's active movements or a case of nervous butterflies. No. Not butterflies—*bats*. Bats on crack.

When the fluorescent lights flicked back on at the end of this informative little film, Jayson glanced at my face and then widened his eyes with faint alarm. "You OK?" he whispered in my ear.

"Nope," I whispered back. He later told me that he'd never seen my face so ghostly white. I'm sure I had never felt so frail and afraid. Nor had I ever felt my fear lead so immediately to resentment.

I started to feel bitter on behalf of all the nameless heroines whose flesh had torn and whose lives had ended in order to bring forth the men whose names would go down in history for having escaped battle without so much as a paper cut. *Hail, mighty men of valor.* Meanwhile, the ladies—if they are mentioned at all—seemed to get the historical equivalent of a participation ribbon. Was that fair? Was that right? I wasn't just terrified; I was angry and terrified.

My fear, at root, was a spiritual problem that was all tied up with selfishness and a growing bitterness toward

God for my lot in life as a woman. This kind of fear was built on an unacknowledged distrust of God's handling of my story. Of all the stories. Rather than standing in awe of Him, I was attempting to stand in judgment over Him whose very breath I borrowed to voice my complaints.

Rather than letting my thoughts and feelings about motherhood begin with the fear of *God*, they began with a fear of just about everything else. Fear became the warped glass through which I peered out at the world, distorting whatever I saw or heard or felt. My head could assent to the neatly packaged theological proposition that children are a blessing and that God's promises are true. My heart, however, was a roiling black cauldron of bitterness and terror. In the grip of these bouts of dread, my throat would tighten, and I could hear the *whoosh-whoosh* of my own racing pulse in my ears. I could hardly speak. And speechlessness usually means prayerlessness.

So long as I could bury the thought of labor and delivery underneath other distractions, I was able to function almost normally. I kept busy to keep my mind on other things. But as the prospect of birth came more frequently to mind, fear's choke hold kept me from speaking about it to anybody, least of all to my God.

"The sacrifice is so worth it!" smiling women had assured me. But now, as my belly grew, my confidence in this assertion had shriveled. The sacrifice part I could still understand. It was, in fact, the *only* part I seemed to understand. It was the "worth it" part that was so hard to believe.

Honestly, the memory of this internal turmoil is something I'd rather keep to myself. These memories pain me, and to write about them—to expose them to public scrutiny—is genuinely mortifying. But what I hope to do is not to revel in the fear and brokenness so that we can all commiserate and make peace with the mess but to dig out the root of that selfish fear and to kill it right where it grows.

NONE OF US SHOULD BE IN THE LEAST BIT surprised that female fertility is at the center of some of our fiercest cultural battles. It is also at the center of many women's fiercest internal and spiritual battles. The ability to bear children is simultaneously an awesome strength and an awful vulnerability—an unparalleled superpower that can bring us to our knees.

Pregnancy and motherhood can present more temptations to fear and despair than I can name, so it seems unlikely that *I* could have been the only happily married middle-class conservative Christian woman who has given way to fear and dread over the thought of giving birth to a child.

And, sadly, given the decades-long bloodbath that we have witnessed since *Roe v. Wade*—across the whole economic, ethnic, marital, and, yes, even religious

spectrum of our society—it's also very, very likely that
at least a few of these women have let that fear lead
them to the knife. Fear, in fact, appears to be the abortion industry's most powerful selling point, which is
one of the reasons I felt compelled to bring this ugly
chapter of my experience to light.

To a woman who is pregnant and scared, "Care, no
matter what" (Planned Parenthood's slogan) *is* what she
most wants, but fear can drive her to look for it in the
worst of places. The voices from the abortion industry
are masters at giving fear a megaphone and turning up
the volume until it drowns out everything else: *What will
happen to your friendships? Your reputation? Your education?
Your body image? Your love life? Your money? Your career? It
will all fall into ruins unless you allow us to cut away the
source of these fears!*

These champions of "choice," adept at convincing
pregnant young women that there *is* no choice, offer only
one way to end the fear: bloodshed. But when fear leads
to bloodshed, bloodshed also leads to guilt—something
that cannot be crushed and extracted with surgical instruments. And the guilt, as many post-abortive women
have discovered, gives birth to new and weightier fears
that rush in to take the place of the old. Who, dear lady,
will care for you—"no matter what"—now? There is no
government-subsidized clinic, no pink-hat street rally,
no fundraiser fun run to assist you.

I'm grateful that, even on my worst days, the abortion "solution" was never one I considered, though my fear and lack of faith were the same root sins of those who have. I refused to believe in the promises offered by my "right to choose," but despite the lip service I gave to God's kindness and sovereignty, I was refusing to rest in His promises. I felt that I had already surrendered quite enough of my own painless, predictable plans to His, thank you very much. So why was He demanding this, too? Couldn't this quiet life, this painless existence, this familiar, comfortable body be mine and mine alone? God was meddling with something that I desperately wanted to control. (*My body. My choice.* Sound familiar?)

This kind of fear is clearly not unique to me, and it's true that we do need a solution to it. We *need* our fear and guilt and shame to be washed away. It's also true that the only thing that can finally wash it away is the blood of an innocent victim. The abortion peddlers got at least that part of the story right. The question, then, is not *whether* innocent blood is necessary but *whose*?

Unlike those who are offering the other "solution," Christians do not hide the bloodiness of their answer behind clinical language or pink signs or tidy code words. How could we? The blood of Christ is not a political platform. It is our life. It is not pink; it is red as wine. Only when we find forgiveness in Him and lay the weight of our faithless fears at His feet do we finally find the perfect care we are seeking—care no matter what. Only His yoke is easy. Only His burden is light.

WHY, I WONDER, IS IT SO EASY TO FORGET how great God's kindness is toward His children? For us who know Him, it's almost always a failure of memory that has led to a failure of nerve.

God has warned us so many times not to forget Him, not to forget His words, not to forget His works. And yet we do it all the time. We should never kid ourselves into thinking that we're really all that different from the people of Israel panicking on the very brink of the beauty and abundance of the promised land. Like them, we know the mighty works of God—that He can create the universe with a word and reduce empires to ashes with a breath—but when we see that there are "giants" in the land, suddenly we forget everything we've witnessed, and we sound the retreat and try to run away from the very blessings He has offered, through faith, to give us. At least, that's what I did. There I was, pregnant—on very border of this great blessing—and I was telling myself that childbirth was too big an obstacle for the God who rules the nations and raises the dead.

I WISH I COULD SAY THAT ON ONE MOMENTOUS day before Jonah, my first child, was born, I suddenly came to my senses and turned my fears over to God. But I didn't. I was afraid right up until the day I went into labor.

The labor itself was long, but nothing terrible, and after I had been carried safely through, I should have been swept away by gratitude and relief, but given how poorly I'd prepared to receive the joy set before me, I remained miserable for weeks.[1]

It took many hours of intense prayer, lots of Psalm reading, countless hard-fought battles against self-pity, and constant words of encouragement from my husband as well as quiet moments of simply recognizing, to my astonishment, the image of God in my son, before the fear and bitterness started to wane. It took sheer divine mercy before I began to embrace cheerfully the incredible gift that I, blinded by my own self-centeredness, had so begrudgingly received.

It was my husband who first noticed that a change was underway.

One day, when Jonah was still only a few months old, he contracted an illness that made it impossible for him

1 This is not at all to downplay the overwhelming physical and hormonal shifts that take place before, during, and after birth, or to dismiss postpartum depression as a mere attitude problem. Our bodies and souls are linked in ways that require a great deal of wisdom to address, and I will not attempt to do so here. But I will say this: seeking *both* Christian counsel *and* medical expertise—something I wish I'd done far more of—during the months following childbirth has been a tremendous help for many, many women and should not be overlooked if motherhood becomes misery. Even letting a friend or a grandparent babysit for just long enough to take a nap and a hot shower can make a hard day much sweeter, so don't try to go it alone.

to keep down any fluids. He was feverish and almost too sick to cry, so I held him in my arms and cried for him. Not for me. Not for all the extra laundry he was making. Not for my wasted efforts at feeding him. Not for worries over how we'd pay the doctor bill if it came to that. No. I broke down in tears because I loved my son and hated to see him suffer. When Jayson saw my tears and I told him what was wrong, he pointed out to me the significance of this change; it had happened so gradually that I'd missed it.

I *loved* my son—not myself through him, but him, himself. And, somehow, along the way, my fear and resentment over the loss of my old way of life had been smoldering and burning away, like dross.

This, I've found, is how God often works—not in a blinding flash but in a slow and subtle transformation that cannot be perceived by the naked eye, like watching a garden grow. Fear could be replaced with hope only when I was finally willing to see my life, with all its petty ambitions, as a seed. I could try to lock it up, worrying that it might get dirty, or wet, or—worse—*buried*. But to fear those things it to forget what a seed is for.

Fifteen years ago, God knew all about my self-centered, cotton-candy plans, and He saw fit to toss them in a puddle, let them dissolve, and give me something of real substance in their place. He took a look at my tidy blueprints for my life and lit them on fire. It all sounds so harsh. So heartless. But I think I can now safely say that there is no one I pity more than the one whose life goes exactly according to her own plans.

In spite of my shallow desires, God gave me my first-born son—once, as I teetered fearfully on the brink of life, and a second time, years later, as he was pulled back from the terrifying brink of death. And God has given my son his own story of being recalled to life again—life that is of more value than many sparrows (Matt. 10:31).

CHAPTER 2

Car(apace)

W hen Jonah, our first child, was just two months
old, we packed our scant belongings and moved
across the country to Irving, Texas, for my husband to
pursue a graduate degree. Two years of studies for a master's degree became five years of studies for a PhD, and
in that time two more sons, Jude and Paul, were added
to our crew. We look back fondly on the friendships we
made there and on the ways that God helped us to grow,
not just in number but spiritually and intellectually as
well. So when our family finally returned to Idaho after
five years of life in the South, we knew that we were returning as changed people who would need to readjust

to the Idaho pace of life. We also knew that we'd need to reacclimate to the cold of the northern winters.

"Reacclimate" may not even be the right word for it. Despite having spent most of my upbringing in north Idaho, I'm not sure I ever really adjusted to the winter weather. We knew we'd miss those Dallas Januaries. What we hadn't realized was how expensive that change in seasons would be. Snow suits and parkas and gloves and boots and car seat covers and ice scrapers and snow shovels added up quickly. But snow tires were an expense that we, with our meager grad-student budget, had a very hard time justifying. So we put it off.

Even after two years of sliding gracefully through stop signs and spinning in place while attempting to exit our well-glazed parking space, my husband and I had continued to question the necessity of a new set of snow tires. Every time a little snow fell, we'd start to lean toward making that huge purchase, but then the snow would melt back into rain, and we'd breathe a sigh of relief that we'd avoided the unnecessary expense.

Between light dustings of snow, we'd discuss the folly of spending all of our pitiful savings versus the folly of driving without traction. Was it *really* worth hundreds of dollars just to be able to stop when we wanted to stop or go when we wanted to go? Then came the first genuine snowfall in November, which sent us van-skiing down a steep hill toward a busy intersection right in the middle of our small town's rush-minute traffic. That thrilling brush with disaster ended the debate. We wanted to live through another winter. So we slimmed down our bank account, handed over a hefty chunk of our savings to the hardworking folks at Les Schwab Tire Co., and drove away, accompanied by the reassuring crunchity-crunchity-crunch of metal studs against ice.

It's a purchase we have not regretted since. Even so, I'm always grateful for an excuse to stay off the roads when the snow starts to fall.

WHEN I WAS A KID, I USED TO ENJOY WINTER travel, usually because it meant spending Christmas with my multitudes of cousins. Long road trips were always as much a part of our holiday traditions as Grandma Kvale's roast turkey, Uncle Ken's eggnog lattes, and the distinctive *hyill-hyill-hyill* of Aunt Marilynn's laughter emanating from the kitchen. Each year, my parents, my brother, and I opened our gifts early and then piled into our boxy Toyota Tercel wagon for the drive across the state of Washington to my grandparents' house on the hill.

As we neared our destination in the evening after six hours of sharing the back seat with my little brother, I would watch expectantly through the window for the brightly lit star that my grandfather always set atop the roof of their home—high enough to be seen from the interstate.

When we finally arrived at the house, I loved to run up the spiral staircase to the guest bedroom. From there, through the age-rippled window glass, I could glimpse ten thousand red brake lights and ten thousand white headlights forming a peaceful rolling stream along Tacoma's Interstate 5 below. After experiencing the speed and intensity of city traffic, the transformation seemed surreal. As bright and cheerful as a string of Christmas lights, rows of cars, trucks, and buses glistened under the pink-orange glow of the sodium vapor street lamps. Who, with that bird's-eye view, would consider the possibility that tragedy might, at any moment, interrupt that grace-ful slow dance through the fog?

EVERY CHRISTMAS OF MY CHILDHOOD HAD sent us weaving our icy way around the Palouse hills, through the Columbia Gorge, over the mountain passes (chains or snow tires required), and along roadways blasted out of the granite walls with countless sticks of dynamite. We zipped through snow and ice and rain at historically unprecedent-ed speeds, passing mere feet from other vehicles that raced along at equally breathtaking velocities. One unexpected bump, one careless flick of the wrist, one brief error in judg-ment, and goodbye family, goodbye beating hearts.

Like most children, I never gave the road conditions so much as a second thought. I had implicit trust in my father's driving abilities and never once suspected that there might be the slightest hint of danger in all that winter driving—not with my dad behind the wheel. Deep in the recesses of my mind lay an early memory of our brand new car being struck by an elderly lady's land yacht, but that did not shake my firm belief that accidents were distant events that happened in other places to other people.

My first true encounter with the hazards of winter travel didn't come until I was a teenager. We were driving home to Idaho after a Christmas in western Washington when, due to an impassable blizzard, we were forced to spend New Year's Eve in an Ellensburg motel. As we set out along an ice-encrusted Interstate 90 the next day, we found ourselves watching in tense amazement as the pickup truck immediately in front of us slid laterally across three lanes of holiday traffic, started into a slow-motion spin, ricocheted off the median, struck another car, and then slipped, missing us by what seemed like inches, into the shallow ditch next to the freeway.

That's when I began to wonder if there was, perhaps, something slightly unsafe about that annual trek over the ice and through the mountains. Even the best of drivers can do nothing to prevent black ice, or drunk college students, or wildlife crossings. (I once watched my brother's Suburban collide, in an explosion of feathers, with a large bird of prey.) Scary things happen on the road—things that no amount of seat belting and defensive driving can control.

Every time we go rolling merrily along the highway, regardless of the weather, we are defying sudden and violent death. Driving is risky—particularly if you live in a college town like mine, where roughly a third of the population consists of young, impatient, inexperienced, and irresponsible drivers. Who of us *doesn't* have a few dramatic car crash (or near-miss) stories to tell?

Just a few months ago, a speeding car ran a red light and nearly collided with me as I was on my way home from my boys' school. And while I was in college, I had not one but *two* cars totaled by inattentive seventeen-year-old drivers in the same year.

I have spent a blazing hot afternoon stranded in a fallow field next to a highway in central Washington with my radiator punctured by a rusty, half-buried tiller—and with only a three-hundred-pound Spanish speaking junk collector and his Great Dane to keep me company. I've had friends hospitalized after being struck by incautious and intoxicated drivers. I've attended the funeral of a young man who fell asleep at the wheel on his way home from the university. One of my college friends lost her new husband to a wintertime car crash. The lives of the sister, brother-in-law, and baby nephew of one of my high school classmates were taken all at once by a drunk driver. My son's classmate lost her life to an icy patch of highway just a few days after Christmas. Limbs and hearts have been broken on nearly every roadway in America. And aside from the terrible human cost of driving, there are all kinds of animal casualties as well. Fifteen years ago, on a trip from New Orleans to Monroe, Louisiana, my husband and I drove past countless dead dogs, cats, possums, turtles, and even small alligators—a veritable natural history museum of roadkill—that had sought high ground on the roadway during a tropical storm. I know multiple people who have struck deer on the highway. The streets where we live are perpetually polka-dotted with crushed squirrel carcasses. In any case, as long as we persist in our driving habits, all sorts of traumatic events are likely to occur on every highway and byway our tires will touch.

But I, just like everybody else, plan to be back behind the wheel today without a second thought. Most of us, I realize, would rather not revert to the old covered wagon routine for bringing home the weekly mountain of groceries, let alone for heading *across* the mountains to visit grandma—especially during the winter months.

Driving is a luxury that most of us really cannot live without—not even at our own peril. And it is perilous. Not to sound panicky or anything, but you could die out there.

As a mom, I read and hear a lot of buzz about the terrible risks we take with our kids when we vaccinate them, or don't vaccinate them, or feed them foods tainted with high fructose corn syrup, or expose them to chemical pesticides, or (perish the thought) let them catch a breath of second hand smoke. But honestly, I suspect that all of those potential dangers pale in comparison to the kind of overt danger we face just driving our little ones to the mall, let alone across hundreds of miles of frozen freeway on a January day.

According to the National Highway Traffic Safety Administration, around 4,400 American children died— and tens of thousands more were injured—in 2015 alone, as a direct result of motor vehicle accidents.[2] Traffic accidents kill roughly seven times more people in a single year in this country than the total number of U.S. military deaths (combat- and non-combat-related combined) in Iraq during the decade from 2003 to 2013.[3] And if these grim statistics were associated with *anything* else—a drug or a chemical or a tainted food product—you can probably imagine the nationwide outcry against it.

But the thing is, even after hearing all about the risks, *we're* the ones voluntarily buckling our very own children into our minivans everyday. We're too busy stressing out

2 National Highway Traffic Safety Administration, "Persons Killed, by Age - State : USA, Year : 2015," https://www-fars.nhtsa.dot.gov/People /PeopleAllVictims.aspx.
3 U.S. Dept of Defense Casualty Report, https://web.archive.org/web /20130116062321/http://www.defense.gov/news/casualty.pdf.

about the trans-fats that the children in the back seat are absorbing from their drive-through fries to think about the death-defying means we took to arrive at the drive-through in the first place. Have we lost our minds? Why aren't we more afraid?

"Perfect love casts out fear" (1 John 4:18). But, as C.S. Lewis points out, "so do several other things—ignorance, alcohol, passion, presumption, and stupidity."[4] Maybe our lack of fear is evidence not of love and noble courage but of thoughtless idiocy with a driver's license. Honestly, now that my son is learning to navigate the family car through our town's chaotic four-way stops, I'm beginning to suspect that this may very well be the case. Defensive driving seems to be the only kind of driving we do. And yet we're not even slightly tempted to give it up.

Driving is, frequently, a mere matter of convenience. Even when walking or biking is a viable option, we choose driving as a quicker and easier way to get from point A to point B. Sometimes we're just lazy.

But often, driving is not a matter of convenience but of necessity. Those of us with multiple kids and multiple gallons of milk to haul across town need some kind of vehicle to help. We also drive out of a sense of obligation. Because modern transportation has made it possible to visit distant friends and family, we feel that we must.

---

4 C.S. Lewis, *The World's Last Night: And Other Essays* (San Diego: Harvest, 2002), 109.

Nobody with a functioning vehicle and some money for gas can legitimately say, "Sorry, Grandma. A hundred miles is just too far to travel for Christmas."

In spite of the obvious dangers, most of the population isn't hitting the road in search of an adrenaline rush. Quite the opposite, actually. I'm not naming any names, but I know some people who actually like to take a drive to *relieve* stress. There is, in fact, a whole genre of driving-for-the-love-of-it songs, and even I can be carried away by that free-wheelin' feelin' of watching the yellow center stripes flick past to the rhythm of a good-mood soundtrack. You just better hope that a stray moose doesn't wander across your path while you're letting the "wind take your troubles away."

That brings me to what might be one of the central reasons for our automobile habit: it makes us feel free. "A car in every driveway" is still very much part of the American dream, and individual autonomy is arguably the reigning American value. According to American Public Media, the city of Los Angeles is home to nearly twice as many cars as drivers. It sounds ludicrous, but for us Americans, a car is more than a tool; it is a status symbol. It is more than a status symbol; it is an extension of who we are. To own a car is to hold a sense of power, independence, and importance. We select the time of departure. We set the speed. We choose the music. We decide where to go, and when to stop, and why. We are kings and queens ruling over our own little steel-and-rubber worlds. This might explain why sweet little old ladies can turn into cussing hussies when they get behind the wheel; on the highway we are tiny independent states vying for dominance, and pity the brazen fool who attempts to invade our territory. ¡Vivà la vehicle!

So, while we may drive for convenience, necessity, pleasure, and the grand illusion of freedom, I have to wonder if even these motivations, powerful as they are, can fully explain our decision to accept the risks involved. Why are we so overwhelmingly willing to play the odds?

THE ODDS THEMSELVES ARE, OBVIOUSLY, PART of the answer. Even in the wintertime, you're not statistically likely to die on the way to grandma's house. For every trip that ends in a deadly crash, there are a million more that reach their destination in perfect safety. The bet is a fairly safe one. But that doesn't change the fact that it's our lives that are on the line, and that we all can remember names of those who have died. Even if there are a million empty chambers in the revolver, Russian roulette is still the game we're choosing to play. (C'mon, kids! Give it a spin!)

Why not stay off the roads whenever possible? Even if the odds are low, why take the gamble when the stakes are so high? For many, ignoring the risks and trusting blind fate are the best reasons they can offer. But for me the overarching reason is probably best summed up in a quote that I've heard attributed to General Stonewall Jackson: "My religious belief teaches me to feel as safe in battle [or behind the wheel] as in bed. God has fixed the time for my death. I do not concern myself about that, but to be always ready, no matter when it may overtake me."[5]

In other words, the risks we take are never governed by impersonal chance. They are never automatic or meaningless. Which is to say, they are not, in the ultimate sense, risks at all; every outcome was fully planned before we were born.

God is the one who holds our lives in His hands. If He didn't, there would be no reason to pray before we travel. If He didn't, it would be perfectly understandable to spend a life locked indoors, wearing a crash helmet and popping vitamins. Instead, I can spend my life driving my kids to baseball practice, visiting friends, and hauling groceries with the confidence that comes from faith: Yea, though I drive through the turnpike of the shadow of death, I will fear no evil, for Thou art with me.

However, we are not called to express our faith by being stupidly suicidal or extreme in our behavior, but by living each day as we ought, loving Him and loving our neighbors, in spite of the apparent dangers. He uses

5 Spoken to Captain John D. Imboden, *Battles and Leaders of the Civil War: being for the most part contributions by Union and Confederate officers, condensed and arranged for popular reading* (New York: The Century, 1894), 1:122-123.

indirect means—from Roman crosses to seat belts—to accomplish His ends. There is no contradiction between trusting God and buying a set of studded snow tires. We can pray for protection, and then we can hit the road, assured that in God's hands we are just as safe—or just as doomed—as we would have been had we stayed home in bed.

Maybe we Christians are willing to accept the danger of driving because we just try not to think about it. But I hope there is more to it than that. I hope that we are accepting the risks of the road because we have taken wise precautions and because we trust God's providence when we get behind the wheel. It seems that we do tend to understand this when it comes to driving, but not when it comes to so much else. I'm not sure why that is, but I *am* sure that we should face *all* the things that we tend to worry about—the way we eat, the way we exercise, the way we vote, the way we raise our kids, and so on—with the same confidence and the same care with which we approach driving: buckle in, follow the rules of the road, and pray for God's sustaining hand to guide you safely through.

So, while purchasing an expensive new set of snow tires was part of being a good steward of our family's lives, and while I may be grateful to stay safely at home for Christmas these days, there is, perhaps, no better time than during the Christmas season to recognize that evading death is not the point of living. This life is not meant to be lived for the sole purpose of its own preservation. That momentous birth in Bethlehem was all about taking up a mortal life in order to lay it down. Because of this, we are free to take risks, even deadly ones, in order to fulfill our duties and in order to love others—which is, when you think about it, essentially the same thing. So over the river and through the woods to grandmother's house we go.

CHAPTER 3

Considering Lilies
and Cleaning Closets

Money, for my family, was tight through most of my childhood, especially when I was very young. My parents worked hard, saved carefully, and managed to put both me and my brother through private Christian school on their modest income, but we rarely had cash left over for luxuries. We never went hungry, but we also seldom ate anything that wasn't bought on sale or wore anything that came new from a department store, either. While other girls my age all seemed to be wearing Guess® jeans, pulling colorfully wrapped Fruit Roll-Ups® from their lunch boxes, and planning to go to Disneyland®

over the summer, for me it was Goodwill, apple slices, and grandma's house.

My dad spent many of my early years finishing his graduate degree and then eking out a living on a lone teaching salary, and my mom knew how to stretch a dollar as well as anyone I've met. Her careful spending also managed to keep us out of debt. I remember sitting in the car with her after grocery runs, waiting while she double checked her receipt for accidental over-charges, and then marching back into the store for a refund on cans of olives that had been rung up at twenty cents more than the listed sale price. She could pinch a penny until it shone like a dime, and those habits served us well through some very lean years.

I was never more grateful for my mom's example of frugality than when my husband began graduate school himself, and I had to put every last nickel to honest work. Living, as they say, paycheck to paycheck, required a lot of coupon clipping and creativity. It also presented a regular temptation to fear for the future—a temptation to worry about tomorrow, what we will eat or what we will drink, or about our bodies, what we will put on (Matt. 6:25). We couldn't afford health insurance, for example, so having two more babies left me biting my nails over the possibility of birth complications and childhood illnesses. And even when the paychecks eventually grew, the concerns over money did not necessarily shrink in an equal and opposite direction.

Nevertheless, that five-year period of surviving below the poverty line taught me to pray earnestly for God to provide, and, in all those years, we seemed to have had our needs met like Israel had in the wilderness; provisions seemed to fall as if from heaven, and, like Israel's clothes and sandals that did not wear out throughout their wanderings (Deut. 29:5), our car did not break down, neither did our computer or health fail during our Texas sojourn. I truly cannot explain how we lived so well on so little, but I was grateful.

Little did I know then *how* grateful I would one day be for the way this experience helped prepare me to look for God's pattern of constant care during times when we might least expect to find it.

NOT LONG AGO, MY HUSBAND AND I SPENT several hours sorting through our jam-packed garage, and we managed to fill an entire pickup truck full of small furnishings, excess shoes, old decorations, and forgotten toys that had been stacked for months in storage containers, awaiting a summer yard sale that never happened. It felt good to deposit the contents of those plastic bins at the local Christian thrift shop. And it felt even better knowing that I was cleaning house for a good cause.

Yes, it felt good. But as nice as it was to open up some closet space, and as useless as those goods are to me now,

I still had a voice in the back of my head telling me that each thing I was giving away might yet prove valuable, might come back in fashion, might fit me again. I've always been a pack rat. My blood pressure rises a bit when I relinquish anything that has the remotest possibility of future utility. *Shouldn't I keep it just in case? What if I can't afford to replace it when I need it?*

I (and my mother and most of my aunts, uncles, and cousins) grew up with a "waste not, want not" outlook on housekeeping. We are still the kind of people who are known to wash and reuse disposable freezer bags. My grandparents, who, just like many of your grandparents, lived through the financially strapped years of the Depression and World War II, went on to raise nine children on a little dairy farm that eventually went bankrupt.

As you can imagine, my grandmother did as much as she could with what little she had, while my grandfather spent much of his time jerry-rigging an assortment of appliances and machinery to avoid having to replace them. Now, I know that the whole "life-changing magic" of throwing away anything that doesn't "spark joy" is hugely popular right now. It's also hugely upper middle class. Poor people usually don't hang onto excess stuff because it brings them *joy*; they hang onto excess stuff because they know it brings them a small sense of financial security—because they know that they could not possibly buy a new one, of whatever it is, once it's gone. Better to keep it as insurance against hard times ahead. My grandpa kept a little collection of broken implements so that he could use them for parts in case some of his functional machinery broke down. Frugality isn't just spending less; it's throwing out less, too. And, for my grandparents especially, frugality was a means of survival. Frugality also seems to have remained in our blood on that side of the family.

Shortly before I was married, one of my mom's dish sponges tore in half. It wasn't one of those "expensive" ones with the scrubby stuff on one side. Nope. Just a basic, fifty-cent yellow dish sponge. But it had scarcely had the chance to perform its humble duty before being rent in two by a bread knife. The average American would, I think, have sent it to an early grave in the city landfill without a twinge of regret. But we are not the average American.

My mom set to work restoring that sponge to the life for which it was intended; she took a needle and some sturdy gray thread, and with nurse-like care stitched the torn halves back together. And when that sponge got dirty, did she throw it out? Oh, no. She sent it through the laundry and then brought it back for *another* round of kitchen patrol next to the sink. When no longer fit for kitchen service, it did time in the bathroom. How long it remained in this degraded position, I don't know. But in the end, worn, tired, and scarred, it took a ride to its final resting place amongst the tuna cans, banana peels, and spent coffee grounds of our fair city. However, none can say that it met an untimely demise. Not at our house.

It's not that any of us thinks we're still living through the Depression. The lean years have passed, but the habit of frugal living hasn't. While my parents have always been careful with money, they keep an open hand and a generous spirit. My mother, who might sew a fifty-cent sponge back together one day, will the next day be cheerfully giving to charity or preparing lovely meals to give to people she's never met. Her frugality and her generosity do not conflict; if anything, her frugality has made her generosity possible. I hope that someday the same could be said of me.

I may not have inherited quite the same degree of waste-nottishness as my mother did, but enough of it remained in the gene pool that I still tend to hang on to things that most people would throw out in a heartbeat. When loading up boxes to donate to a school rummage sale, I nearly kept an out-of-date, hand-me-down baby blanket that none of my kids had ever used. It had no aesthetic value. It had no sentimental value. It had no current practical value. Its only value was in the *just in case* of the thing—*just in case* I have another baby and our thirty-four other baby blankets get ruined before the child outgrows them. Ridiculous, I know.

I, of all people, should realize that, on the day when *just in case* actually arrives, we will have all we need—and probably much more. I have never asked for bread and been given a stone. So why should I be afraid?

When we lived in Dallas, our annual household income (including our "income" from student loans) was well below the federal poverty line for a family of five. I just revisited our tax returns from that time period, and I have no logical explanation for how we got by, let alone for how we lived so comfortably. Not even my überfrugality seems to account for it. The figures, really and truly, don't add up, and I cannot understand how we did not starve or go homeless. But the figures didn't add up the time when that boy handed over his five loaves and two fish to feed the crowd, either. The math was all wrong. Economists would have drawn up disheartening line graphs. Statisticians would have predicted significant food shortages. And yet, there were leftovers. Twelve baskets full.

When we finally packed for our move back to Idaho, I gathered up box after heavy box of our worldly goods from our small Dallas apartment. We filled a huge moving van from front to back. And even then, with nearly all our belongings boxed up and out of reach, we continued to live in relative comfort and ease. One pan to cook with. Cheap paper plates to eat on. A few changes of clothes to wear. Running water. A roof over our heads. We lacked for nothing. The experience made me see how much of a luxury all those other things were that I thought I needed.

Even years later, our household income remained many thousands of dollars below the federal "low income limit" for our county. I was stunned when I saw the numbers. True, we weren't planning to buy a vacation home in Bermuda anytime soon. But we drank wine. We ate well—almost *too* well. Our kids attended a private school. Our clothes were clean and comfortable. Even the dusty corners of our home were filled with toys, games, tools, clothes, gadgets, luxuries . . . . *Low income? Really?*

Of course there were numerous times when finances *were* especially tight, and I really was tempted to fret over money. One day we had to write a check for a hundred dollars that I knew we simply couldn't afford. And after praying that God would provide, we sent it off. The next day a check arrived for (yes, I know, it's just that good) a hundred dollars from a distant relative-by-marriage with a card congratulating my husband on finishing his degree (even though he hadn't yet finished). Not even *I* could have the audacity to believe that the timing of that gift was mere coincidence.

IN THE SEVENTEEN YEARS THAT MY HUSBAND and I have been married, we have given away, sold, or donated hundreds of belongings, and I'm sure I could clear out several more boxes of excess stuff at this moment without noticing the slightest change in the way we live.

Even at our poorest, our "low income" American family had more stuff than we could possibly use. We were wealthy enough to just give things away. If I decided to count my blessings, to name them one by one—even if I limited myself to counting material blessings only—I would have no time for doing anything else.

It's good to look around the room, even at the clutter currently sitting on my desk—my phone, a couple of camera lenses, a stack of books, computer equipment, a full mug of coffee—and count how many of them I could live entirely without. These things that surround me are just a thick layer of buttercream on the hundred-layer cake of pure grace that I've landed in through no merit of my own.

Even if I never find myself sewing a dish sponge back together, I will probably always be somewhat frugal. I am my mother's daughter. But I hope that, like her, that I will also approach my saving and spending with a sense of gratitude and with the knowledge that I am, quite literally, *rich*. Rich in every way.

Through all the years that my grandparents struggled to feed their family, God provided. Through the years that my parents wrung a living out of a meager salary, God provided. Through the years when my own little family was a statistic on the roles of America's "poor," God provided—far beyond what we needed. And years later, the day after the financial bottom dropped out, and we had no idea how we would cover the medical bills that would soon be pouring in, we opened our mailbox to find an unmarked envelope with a small stack of high-denomination dollar bills stuffed inside. We still don't know who gave it to us, and it was only the first of literally hundreds of generous gifts and acts of love that carried us through the hardest days our family has yet faced—without a single concern for our financial needs.

So why waste any more time worrying about the "just in case" scenarios? Haven't I seen how the goodness of God shines brightest in the dark? Haven't I seen how He clothes the wildflowers and feeds the ravens? Why should I fear tomorrow? Better to consider the lilies and start clearing out the closets. They'll be filling up with Christmas gifts again anyway before I know it.

CHAPTER 4

Staying Afloat

This week, I drove a vanload of my boys and their friends down to the local swimming pool and dropped them off for a couple hours of fun in the water, and it brought to mind once again how quickly they are growing up. All the clichés about time are true. It does fly. And it also swims. It seems like just moments ago that I was sitting on the edge of the shallow end watching them learn to overcome their fear and to put their faces under the water for the first time. And now they simply wave goodbye and plunge into the deep end without a backward glance.

Only a handful of summers ago, when our sons began taking swimming lessons, I was pleased to see how my boys cheerfully braved the cold mornings (forty-eight degrees and drizzle on the first day) and pushed themselves to do what, just days before, had seemed impossible. Watching them, I could feel butterflies in my own stomach as I remembered what it was like to take that first frightening leap into the deep water, and to make that first nerve-wracking trip down the big slide through blind curves and slippery darkness. We all know what it's like to be pushed in over our heads.

As the instructors carried the "pre-tadpole" students, who clung fiercely to their teachers' necks, to the "deep" end of the kiddie pool, one child's panicked shrieks suddenly flew across the bright surface of the water: "Don't let go! Don't let go! It's too deep! I! Caaan't! Swiiiim!" From our deck chairs we parents watched these displays of childish terror with mild amusement. We knew they'd be safe, but they, out there where their feet dangled uselessly above the bottom of the pool, were far from convinced.

Each time, the swim teacher repeated what had become a mantra during these mornings at the pool: "I've got you. You'll be all right. You're not gonna sink." But the wildly kicking legs, the rapid gasps for air and the expression of wide-eyed dread proved that this kid was momentarily deaf to all attempts at persuasion. Until his feet could touch the bottom, he would trust no one and nothing but his gut instincts—which were clearly telling him that he was going to die out there in that four-foot-deep chlorinated abyss. And while I may still chuckle at this kind of frantic behavior, these terrified children are certainly not the only ones overcome at times by panic and a sensation of drowning.

Water is a scary substance. It's no wonder that so many of the great stories of deliverance involve escape through and from water: Noah waiting to rise above the deluge, Moses floating down the Nile to Pharaoh's daughter and later holding out his staff to allow the children of Israel to pass through the water to safety, Jonah plunging to certain death and being saved in the nick of time, the disciples frantically waking Jesus to rescue them from drowning at sea, and Peter growing afraid and beginning to sink, calling out, "Lord, save me!" Who of us, if called, would have stepped out of that boat in the first place?

Water is a blessing that can kill. Is it any wonder that being *in too deep* or *overwhelmed* (capsized by waves) are common expressions for that feeling of bewilderment— of being required to do the impossible?

As our children have grown, and the challenges and responsibilities have grown along with them, my husband and I have both felt ourselves drifting away from the shallow end, nearing the deep water where it looks like we're certain to drown. Each time I feel the water rising, I catch my breath and wonder if this is really a good idea. Can we actually stay afloat with so much to weigh us down? Can we keep our heads above water while balancing five kids, a marriage, friendships, work, heaps of little projects, church responsibilities, community responsibilities, sports, travel, illnesses, and so much more? Can't we just stay in the shallow end for a while and let the water splash around our ankles? Half the time I feel like flailing and hyperventilating like that kid in the swim class. Well-intentioned people may be telling me, "You'll be all right. You're not gonna sink," but all I know is that the bottom is a long way down, and I am anything but buoyant.

I'VE HEARD THAT YOUTH GROUP LEADERS AND marriage counselors use "trust games" as a method for strengthening relationships between individuals. One person must fall backward, arms folded, into the waiting arms of another, trusting that those arms will be there to break the fall—strong enough to save and protect from harm. I admit that I've always found the idea of these games pretty ridiculous. I mean, isn't there a less childish and contrived way to build trust?

Well, maybe there is. But watching kids floundering helplessly in water over their heads each year during swimming lessons has given me a new appreciation for these "trust games." It's easy to laugh at my boys' nervousness—and even at their terror. We know that they have nothing to fear, but they know nothing of the kind.

All that stands between them and death is that pair of waiting arms, ready to catch them when they fall, to pull them up when they're sinking.

I know exactly how they feel. While I may, like them, be tempted to doubt and to start pleading, "Don't let go! Don't let go!" there are others—many others—who have already been out here before me, held up by the strong grace of God, and survived. And I'm sure that they are watching me amusedly from their deck chairs as I splash furiously at the water, feeling my feet lift free from the bottom. They are perfectly certain that I am not going to drown. I, while I was back in the shallows of the kiddie pool, found it easy to believe that, too. It's only now, when I'm being called to venture out into these unfamiliar depths, that I grow afraid.

I'm not walking on water. I'm not even treading water. I'm with Peter, staring not at Christ but at the waves, about to go under and crying, "Lord, save me!"

Several years ago, my middle son, Paul, was learning to brave the depths of the local pool. Even with his life jacket firmly secured around his chest and his teacher's arms waiting just below to catch him, Paul was terrified to jump from the end of the diving board. "Thirteen feet deep. This water is thirteen feet deep," he was thinking. The measurements may have had only vague meaning to his four-year-old mind, but even a four-year-old can see that the water below is a darker, deeper shade of blue than the kiddie pool will allow. All our cheery assurances could not convince him of safe passage through that cobalt expanse, and simply seeing others survive the leap was not proof enough that survival was possible for *him*. My little Paul could no more save himself from thirteen feet of water than fly, and yet his teacher was calling to him to jump.

Shivering with both fear and chill, Paul could not bring himself to step off the end of the diving board. So with a nod from my husband, the other instructor dropped him in. And, wonder of wonders, Paul lived to tell the tale. But even his own escape from a watery grave could not convince him to take that fateful step a second time. This, for him, was a true trust game—and not one that, at this point in his young life, he was willing to play again.

We all know that it's more comfortable back in the shallows. It's easier to believe that we're going to survive when we're sitting on the solid planks of the boat. But if we're called to step away from the edge, to walk out where the blue below us is darker, out where the wind is rising, trust becomes a more difficult matter. We grow fearful. We begin to sink. But if we have been called to do the impossible, to jump into the deep end, to step out of the boat in the midst of the sea, go we must.

"He said, 'Come.' So Peter got out of the boat and walked on the water and came to Jesus. But when he saw the wind, he was afraid, and beginning to sink he cried out, 'Lord, save me.' Jesus immediately reached out his hand and took hold of him, saying to him, 'O you of little faith, why did you doubt?'" (Matt. 14:29-31).

CHAPTER 5

Weak in the Knees

You know those stories that people tell where somebody is described as "going weak in the knees" or when a messenger appears with bad news and suggests that the hearers "might want to take this sitting down"? Those had always seemed like exaggerated figures of speech to me. I mean, who *really* goes all noodle-legged in the face of bad news, after all? Surely, not I.

Of course, I know what it is to be sad or afraid or taken off guard. But I tend to think of myself as a pretty emotionally sturdy person. No Victorian fainting couches or smelling salts necessary. And, despite some moments of weakness during my first months as a mother, if you see tears welling up in my eyes, it's more likely than not to be from hay fever. Or so I've told myself for years.

My seemingly stoical DNA, some say, derives from a rather chilly blend of tight-lipped Englishmen, hard-headed Germans, windblown Scots, and the kind of rugged, sunshine-is-for-sissies northern Europeans who chiseled out a living from the frozen fjords. Stout hearts and dry eyes—that's us. As one author put it, "If I were commissioned to design the official crest for the descendants of emotionally muzzled Vikings everywhere, I would begin by looking up the Latin phrase for 'No thanks, I'm fine.'"[6]

Exactly.

But on the evening of August 20, 2012, when my husband carried home the heavy news that our ten-year-old son, Jonah, had been diagnosed with leukemia, I crumpled onto the bottom step of our family's stairway and sobbed.

All through that evening and for many of the days that followed, I learned what it was to go weak in the knees in the most literal sense—no metaphor about it. Each time a doctor would bring new information, I had to take it sitting down. Every time the phone demanded to be answered, my chest felt squeezed in a vise that gripped tighter with every ring.

My child may die. My precious firstborn son may be taken from us. Everywhere I went, I seemed to feel an unbearable

6 Michael Perry, *Truck: A Love Story.* (New York: HarperCollins, 2006), 159.

weight pressing down on my shoulders—a weight that I could not carry. We were given hefty stacks of informational books and brochures, but I could not open them. I could not allow my eyes to rest on phrases like "mortality rate" and "likelihood of relapse." These were words too heavy for me to lift from the page.

My child may die. Even after five years, it continues to be a weight that I cannot carry. But I have learned that it is also a weight that I *need* not carry. That I do not carry. That is not *mine* to carry at all.

A FEW YEARS AGO, OUR CHURCH STARTED A Sunday school class to teach the Heidelberg Catechism to the children. Week after week my kids would recite from memory the answer to that week's question and would review the answers to the questions that preceded it. This meant that, week after week, the first question would come: *What is your only comfort in life and in death?*

Then a chorus of sing-song treble voices would reply,

> That I am not my own, but belong—body and soul, in life and in death—to my faithful Savior, Jesus Christ. He has fully paid for all my sins with his precious blood, and has set me free from the tyranny of the devil. He also watches over me in such a way that not a hair can fall from my head without the will of my Father in heaven; in fact, all things

must work together for my salvation. Because I belong to him, Christ, by his Holy Spirit, assures me
of eternal life and makes me wholeheartedly willing
and ready from now on to live for him.

It's a long answer. We spent what felt, to the kids, like
ages trying to memorize it. I remember feeling the same
way learning it myself. But in the frightening days that
followed Jonah's diagnosis, those familiar lines that had
rattled around in my own head for so many years and
that had echoed around the walls of the Sunday school
classroom for so many weeks sputtered to life. That dusty
paragraph began lighting up like the county fair at nightfall. I had memorized those antique words and I had
believed them—but never quite so fully. Never quite so
desperately. Never in such bright, neon colors.

Each night as I pleaded with God for Jonah, I pulled
those words, like a lifeline, into my prayers: "Jonah is not
his own. He is not my own. God Almighty, he is Your
child. And nothing can happen to a hair on his head—or
to a blood cell in his body—apart from Your will." And
even in the praying of those words, that suffocating, crippling weight began to lift. Jonah belongs to his faithful
Savior. Body and soul. In life—and, yes, even in death.

Psalms, too, and hymns that I had sung for years
and committed to memory—sometimes without much
thought—were now surfacing in my head and heart and
proving to be both priceless and indispensable. All those

pictures of God as a refuge, as a fortress, as a rock, as a tower, as a physician, as a friend now meant something far more concrete. Here was comfort beyond imagining. Here was peace beyond understanding.

During those first few months of upheaval, Jayson and I regularly spent several days at a time separated from each other. One of us stayed with Jonah at the hospital, ninety miles away, while the other managed the household routines. We had plenty of help with bills and housework, but we did not often have each other to lean on for comfort. During those lonely days and weeks, however, the sturdy old truths stacked on the shelves of my memory became sweeter company than I'd ever imagined they could.

It was as if I, when I was feeling particularly wealthy, had stuffed a large roll of high-denomination bills into my pockets and then forgotten about them. But then, when hard times fell and I thought I was going broke, I put a hand into my pocket and discovered that I was still rich after all; I had everything I needed, and it had appreciated in value.

As I shuffled with Jonah through the halls of the hospital, helping drag his rattling IV pole, trying to look beyond the darkness cast by my own fears, I prayed desperately for help. And the more I prayed, the more I found that the verses I'd committed to memory during my childhood began to catch fire and shine as beacons through this valley of the shadow.

Here were these words, that had seemed at times—especially when I was young and tired of memorizing—to be so much gravel, tossed into my empty little head and tumbled around over the years. But now, here they were again, pouring back out all gleaming and precious and polished smooth—not gravel at all but *rubies.*

"God is our refuge and strength, a very present help in trouble. Therefore will not we fear, though the earth gives way, though the mountains be moved into the heart of the sea" (Ps. 46:1–2). I remembered these lines as a little ditty set to a tune for teenage voices and a solo guitar. But thanks to that simple melody, those words were epoxied into the back pages of my mind such that I never lost them.

Until now, however, I had never deeply considered them.

It's not that I had ever doubted the truth of those words, but I had believed them more or less in the abstract. They existed somewhere in the clouds. Now, however, in the middle of my trouble, with my comfortable little world falling into the sea, those true words came down out of the ether and became the very solid ground beneath my feet. God is a refuge—from fear and death. He is strength—when my knees buckle and I cannot stand. He is a very present help—a right-here-right-now help, a help mediated through comforting words and free babysitting and hot meals and carpool rides and peaceful sleep. He is a help in trouble—in cancer and confusion and grief. Therefore we will not fear. We will not be afraid of this. Not even if the world crumbles around us and cancer does its worst.

THROUGHOUT MY LIFE, MY PARENTS HANDED down to me a greater inheritance of faith than I can enumerate in the pages of a short book. But two of the greatest gifts they gave me were the resources for and the example of how to face trials as a Christian. I lived in a home steeped in the reading of Scripture, where my parents read their Bibles, where my dad read the Word to us at the table or before bed, where books of theology and fat commentaries lined the bookshelves, and where I knew instinctively that this book from God was something to be received, believed, and acted upon daily. We were members of churches that sang Psalms regularly, so that the words sank into my memory in a way they never could have without singing them.

And, while they may have had their moments of anxiety, I cannot remember a time when either of my parents let the phrase, "I'm worried . . . " cross their lips while I was within earshot. Instead they rested in God's promises, did the work at hand, and prayed.

When money was short, they worked hard, tightened the budget, and prayed. When crises arose in the extended family, they sought counsel, began difficult conversations, and prayed. When we found ourselves stranded and in fear for our safety in foreign countries, they locked our doors, looked for a way of escape, and prayed.

I have seen them pray for innumerable things and in innumerable situations. But I have never watched them panic.

How many of us can say that? How many of us, when we were children, have been witness to a full-blown fear-induced parental meltdown? How many kids have watched their mom and dad argue about how they are going to pay the bills or feed the family or deal with a sudden illness? My dad's mother, my grandma Fran, much as I loved her, spent her entire life expressing worry and fear about tomorrow: "I'm just so *worried* about . . . " or "Well, I just don't know what to *do* . . . " She would worry herself (quite literally) sick when my parents would leave for a vacation or when someone in the family fell ill. And my mother would repeat to her—over and over and over, year after year—the words that I have often found myself repeating to my own children (and to myself):

Worrying is not going to help. God knows what we need. Pray about it. Ask God to deal with that situation. Trust Him. Ask Him. Believe His promises.

Yes, my firstborn son was diagnosed with cancer. Yes, the news was a staggering blow, but God had begun preparing me for this day by showing His mercies in a hundred other hard moments and by providing me with parents who knew, deep in their bones, what it was to trust

WEAK IN THE KNEES 57

the Lord in all circumstances. Could I ever have thought to ask for a more gracious gift than that?

Could we ask for a more precious gift to give our own children? Do we ask for such gifts to give our children? My parents not only taught us that our lives were in God's hands; they lived in a way that showed it. They spoke of it. They prayed it. They raised my brother and me with truths from Scripture that could not fail to provide grace in time of need.

And that day—August 20, 2012—was, far and away, our greatest time of need.

THERE'S A QUOTE, ATTRIBUTED MOST FREQUENTLY to the Jamaican reggae musician Bob Marley, that's been circulating through my social media feed lately. Sometimes I see it imposed over a photo of a lone mount climber, sometimes scrawled in brush script over a watercolor painting of flowers, and once, inked across somebody's taut young skin in the form of a fresh tattoo. It says, "You never know how strong you are until being strong is your only choice."

I understand the popularity of the sentiment—that it is meant to inspire us, to help us dig deeper, to hold our heads higher, to puff out our chests, grit our teeth and power through the pain. I'm sure there must be weight lifters and marathon runners who wear this on their T-shirts as inspiration to do *just one more* vein-popping rep, and to take that next excruciating step. I get it. But when "being strong," *all on your own*, is really and truly your only choice—when nothing else is left to you but your own private wellspring of inner fortitude, how strong are you really?

I would submit: *not very*.

I have joked about my family's deep-seated stoicism, and there may be a grain of truth to it. But in reality, I believe that the sort of calm fearlessness I've seen in my family is rooted in something far deeper than stout self-reliance, which turns out to be a rather flimsy platform on which to stand—especially while one's knees are in the process of buckling. It is certainly rooted in something deeper than our stone-cold, stiff-upper-lip Scandinavian DNA.

No, this strength to face the future that I see in my mother and her siblings, and that I saw in her parents, is not stone-cold but rock-hard. It is founded in a hope that is built on the solid rock, the mighty fortress, the strong tower. It is faith that sees the good hand of God at work in all things,[7] and that His power is made perfect not when we discover our inner strength, but when we are at our weakest and most helpless.[8]

7 See Rom 8:28. Everyone will quote this verse at you *ad nauseam* when you're in the midst of a trial. Believe it anyway.
8 See 2 Cor 12:9ff.

To turn Bob Marley's words on their head, *You never know how strong God is until being weak is your only choice.* Through our weakness, we discover the perfect power of God.

THE YEARS OF JONAH'S CANCER TREATMENT have been, without question, the most difficult years of our lives. My son has fought a life-threatening disease. But do I wish this had never happened? Do I wish I could erase the last five years and start them fresh and clean and cancer-free? I hesitate. Strange as it sounds, I don't.

Several people have told me that they just don't think they could do what we've done; that they couldn't handle facing childhood cancer; that it would simply be too hard. And I suppose the expected reply would be, "Oh, no, of course you could! You're a strong person. You could handle it if you had to."

But I'm not always a good cheerleader. In fact, what I generally want to say is, "Yeah, you're right. It *is* too hard. You *couldn't* do it."

The reason I say that, however, is that *I* can't do it either. I can't handle it. Not me. Not our family carrying all this trouble on our own strength. We *didn't* do it. We *didn't* handle it—at least not in some kind of stoical, self-sufficient, inner-strength, no-thanks-I'm-fine kind of way.

Rather, we were helpless. We were weak in the knees. We had to take it sitting down. But God was our strength. We were neck-deep in trouble. But He is a very present help in trouble. We were faced with the fear of death. But our comfort is that we belong, even in death, to our faithful Savior, Jesus Christ. And having seen with my own eyes the unfailing mercy and goodness of God, I am no longer afraid.

Since the battle for Jonah's life began five years ago, we have seen our prayers answered again and again. His hair, his color, and his laughter are back. But the fight for his life is not yet over; we are facing the Last Enemy, even now. Relapse and secondary cancers and long-term health problems remain a real possibility. *My child may die.* Even after all this time, I still can hardly bring myself to say those words aloud, and my throat aches if I try.

But when this race has been run, I hope that my children will have seen in me what I have seen in my mother—a daughter of Sarah: "And you are her children, if you do good and do not fear anything that is frightening" (1 Pet. 3:6).

This has been a time of testing, but this has also been a time in which all those abstract truths that we have always believed truly put on flesh. God's power is made perfect in our weakness. God is our refuge and strength. This is why my knees are steady. This is why that terrible weight is gone.

You have dealt well with your servant,
   O LORD, according to your word.
Teach me good judgment and knowledge,
   for I believe in your commandments.
Before I was afflicted I went astray,
   but now I keep your word.
You are good and do good;
   teach me your statutes. (Ps. 119:65-68)

CHAPTER 6

Cirque du Today

If there was one skill that our whole family had to learn as we dealt with Jonah's cancer, it was flexibility. Every time Jonah's situation changed—and it changed frequently—we had to be ready on a moment's notice to swivel and twist and turn our plans upside-down. Some days I felt like I belonged to a troupe of those gravity-defying acrobats, dangling precariously from a wildly swaying trapeze, my limbs looped all around like a human pretzel. *How did I end up here?* I'd wonder. *Why did I agree to this? It feels like madness. It probably looks like madness, too.* But in reality it was the only sane thing to do. If I were to remain stiff and still—if I had stubbornly refused to take part in that swirling circus act—I would simply have been knocked flat on my back by the force of the action around me. The show, as they say, must go on, whether I participated willingly or not.

I was willing. I truly was. But I was awfully sore.

Before Jonah's diagnosis, we tended to be creatures of ossified habit, usually making plans that required little elasticity and even less variation from our comfortable, predictable routines. But on that startling August day, as we puttered along, adhering to our carefully plotted road-map, we slammed the brakes when our intended path was washed away by a landslide, our map flew out the window, and we were forced to turn down roads we'd never imagined we'd be traveling. Now we sped along through a mind-bending series of detours, reverses, and hairpin curves through unfamiliar spaces where almost anything might be just around the next bend. *Here be dragons.*

We avoided making time-sensitive promises. We RSVPed with caveats. When my birthday popped up on the calendar that fall, we were uncertain where Jonah would be over the weekend, so we waited until the last minute to make a decision about how to celebrate. I was supposed to sign up for a specific date and time for parent-teacher conferences, but I didn't because, well, I had no idea what I'd be doing in two hours, let alone in two weeks. With the help of my church, my parents, my mother-in-law, and many, many friends, we did try to stick to a schedule for the rest of the family, and our other kids adjusted fairly well to the "new normal," but Jonah's situation was a constant question mark looming over each day's activities, and we all sometimes felt stretched a little thin.

I grew weary of answering the seemingly simple question, "So, what are your plans for today/tomorrow/this week?" I just never knew. I was reminded over and over of what the apostle James says: "You do not know what tomorrow will bring. What is your life? For you are a mist that appears for a little time and then vanishes. Instead you ought to say, 'If the Lord wills, we will live and do this or that'" (James 4:14–15). This had, of course, always been true, but it never seemed more obvious. More times than I can count, as soon I told someone our "plans," some unforeseen situation arose to change them. If I informed people that Jonah would receive a blood transfusion that day, he didn't. If I said that Jonah was likely to have a good week, then he would spend the next seven days in bed sleeping or puking. And if I fully expected him to feel terrible after his chemo, then sure enough, he'd be cheerfully sitting up in his bed, enthusiastically talking about baseball, and eating heaps of spicy Thai curry. So who was I to tell anybody my *plans*? I was not writing this story. I was simply living it. And living it in faith meant for me to live it flexibly. Still does.

I tried to keep friends and family up-to-date on Jonah's condition, but just writing those brief updates was a difficult exercise. I would delete more than I published, wondering what tone to take, what details to share. Dwell too long on the struggles and heartaches, and it sounded like an ungrateful pity party. Spend too long giving glowing reports of happy moments, and it read—at least to me—like a cheap veneer. The fact was both sides of this story existed simultaneously. Dark clouds and sunshine shared the same sky.

On the one hand, Jonah appeared to be moving steadily toward recovery. God was helping us to grow and mature, and we had a small army of people praying for us, holding us up, catching us when we fell, and helping us to untangle those acrobatic knots we were tied in. We knew we had been blessed beyond measure. But on the other hand, we had a very sick child missing his friends, missing his routine, missing his health, missing out on school, and fighting a life-threatening disease. We existed in a state of constant flux and sudden change, perpetually living out of suitcases in a no-man's land between hospital, borrowed beds, and home. We had to stay on our toes as much as any prima ballerina, and we were stretched far beyond our comfort zones. We all could definitely feel the burn.

One hour, Jonah would be doubled over with nausea. Then next, the nausea medication started to make him so dizzy he could hardly walk and so loopy he couldn't finish a coherent sentence or remember what he'd done five minutes earlier. Then he might start having abdominal pains. Or complaining of mouth sores. He couldn't face the sight of a muffin, and yet he'd beg for greasy, fiery-hot potato chips. One minute he'd be smiling and making craft projects, and the next he'd collapse onto his back, moaning and clutching his belly. There were many days when I couldn't decide if it was best to make him nap or eat or study or take a walk.

After days spent apart, our family finally planned to spend the weekend together, but when two-year-old Liam got sick the night before, we realized that, in order to protect Jonah's fragile immune system, a family gathering was not going to happen. Plans would change and change and change again. And when they did, we needed to be ready to spin and bend.

I tried to tell myself that, in years to come, we would spend a lot of time laughing over some of the crazy contortions we found ourselves performing during this three-ring circus. But in the dim hallways of the ER, with my son writhing in greater pain than even a morphine drip could alleviate, the happy ending was hard to picture.

When I reach the tense, frightening chapters of a book, before I keep reading, I almost always skip to the last page, just to make sure that everything turns out all right in the end. Plenty of people argue that this ruins the story—that knowing how it ends might not even make it worth reading.

I think they're wrong.

I can concede that spoilers might steal some of the delight of that initial surprise, but if the story is really a great one, then the principle delight comes in seeing *how* all the tightly crafted details work together to lead up to that conclusion. Any story that can't hold up once a spoiler gives away the ending probably wasn't a well-told story in the first place. As my husband likes to point out, the great books only get richer with multiple readings, and, for me, knowing how they end is the incentive I need in order to keep forging ahead through the heart-pounding chapters.

It's no different in this kind of real-life cliffhanger; it's the spoilers that keep me going.

While we may have lost control of a particular scene, our God hasn't. He is writing our story, and He writes well. He writes well even during the suspenseful chapters. Especially during the suspenseful chapters. But knowing that He will set all these wrongs to right is the happy ending "spoiler" that encourages me to turn to the next page.

Corrie ten Boom, the Dutch Christian woman who helped save the lives of dozens of Jews, survived the horrors of a Nazi concentration camp, and lost some of her closest friends and family to the brutality and injustice of the German invaders, often quoted this poem describing life as a tapestry:

Oft' times He weaveth sorrow;
And I in foolish pride
Forget He sees the upper
And I the underside.[9]

I love how well this image captures the sensation of being stuck in a tangled mess and unable to discern the work of art that is coming together, just beyond our line of sight. God is weaving this apparent chaos of loose and twisted fibers into a rich and beautiful design, so I can trust that when, at last, He pulls me, on my own slender thread, through to the other side, the work I will see will be glorious beyond anything we could have dreamed. Even the smallest stitch will have been perfectly, marvelously placed.

While I may not know many of the intervening details that will get us there, I can take courage because I already know that this story ultimately ends well. I can step out from the wings to grab hold of the swaying trapeze, to bend with every plot twist in this particular suspense story, because I know the Author; because I know the Author is good; because I know His promises are true.

9 Quoted in Corrie ten Boom, "The Tapestry," found in *Messages of God's Abundance* (Grand Rapids: Zondervan, 2002), 62.

CHAPTER 7

Flailing

It's easy, I know, to talk about trusting the Author of our life stories when we think we can expect the plot to lead in a straight line from sunshine to roses; *I'll graduate, get happily married, live in a beautiful home, have a fulfilling job, find faithful friends, and have a collection of healthy, happy, above-average children.* But chasing a bright, shiny path into the future is not necessarily the same thing as trusting God's plan for our lives. Sometimes, in fact, it's quite startlingly different.

I once watched a plump, two-inch-long dung beetle fly through the humid East African night air—with a sound like the low buzz of a small, distant aircraft—smack into an outdoor light fixture mounted to a cement wall. The creature fell with a soft thud onto its back, where it lay in the red dirt, legs flailing helplessly. Those of us standing nearby gathered around and watched it for a minute, waiting for it to right itself. It couldn't. It needed a friendly flip from a human toe to turn its fat body right side up. The minute its six legs made contact with solid ground, it once more spread its armored wings, wobbling as it left the ground, and retraced its quixotic path through the air toward the light, where it repeated the same sorry scene: Smack! Thud. Flail, flail, flail. *Flip.* Buzz. Smack! Thud. Flail. Flail. Flail . . .

It was funny. And pitiful. But I have been that dung beetle—more times than I care to admit.

I'll be zipping along at full speed in the confident pursuit of some grand plan (usually the kind made without much prayer or good advice). The future is looking bright, and I imagine that I'm riding off into the familiar sunset. Except that the golden glow I've been flying toward turns out *not* to be the sunset at all but a dead end—as solid and unyielding as a flood lamp anchored to a cinder block wall. Smack! Thud. Flail.

There I lie—disappointed, confused, helpless—until someone lifts me up and sets me on my feet.

Learning that my son had cancer was very much like careening, at full cruising speed, into a wall. The bright future I had imagined for our family was not one that involved this kind of disruption. I thought we had been gliding toward a future that involved the easy predictability I'd come to expect—kids entering school in carefully planned succession, money set aside little by little to buy a house, year upon year of reliable work punctuated with well-planned times of leisure—and interrupted by only the minor sorts of bumps in the road to which I'd grown accustomed: skinned knees, winter sniffles. That sort of thing.

Smack! Thud.

For me, the collision came in the form of pediatric leukemia. For others, it's a death in the family, an injury, the loss of a job, a sudden financial crisis, or something else. But one of the common themes of our fallen race is that God uses these collisions to point us toward Himself. Finding ourselves stunned, flailing, and staring up at the stars can be a great mercy because it does two things: first, it gives us a sudden, clear understanding of our own utter helplessness, and second, it provides us with an opportunity like no other to lift up our eyes to the One from whom our only help comes. There's nothing quite like being knocked flat on my back to point my gaze toward heaven. Unfortunately, some of us (*ahem*), like that dung beetle, must be knocked flat more than once before we willingly seek a different source of light.

SITTING BY JONAH'S SICKBED FOR COUNT-less hours provided me with plenty of time to meditate on our helplessness—on our lack of control over so many of the details of our own lives.

Ninety miles away from the rest of my family, unaware of what activity might be in progress at home, I sat in the recliner next to Jonah's hospital bed, listening to the rhythmic beep of the IV pump and breathing air tinged by disinfectant. In this room, all illusions of self-sufficiency had evaporated as quickly as the rubbing alcohol the nurses used to clean my son's PICC line.

I had no idea what news would be dropped into our laps at any moment. Lab technicians on the opposite side of the country were evaluating the DNA in my son's cancerous blood cells. My mother-in-law had taken over the folding of my laundry. A young woman from our church was scrubbing my toilets. People I hardly knew were cooking our meals. Families I didn't know at all were sending us cards and offering their prayers on our behalf. And I could do nothing—nothing—to turn back the clock or heal my son of this life-threatening disease. I couldn't even pack my children's school lunches. In these circumstances, how could I not recognize my utter dependence upon my God, and upon the people with whom He had surrounded us?

So often, I respond to life's small crises by getting to work—by *doing* something about the problem. But here, for hours and days at a time, I had nothing at all I could do but wait and pray and ride out the storm. I could not chart a new course, set a better sail, or steer this vessel in a new direction. I was not the captain of this ship any more.

I never had been.

OUT OF THE MILLION MOMENTS THAT MAKE up my life, is there a single one to which I can point and say, "That was all *me*. *I* planned that. *I* made that happen"?

I did not even choose to be born. I had no say over my family. I was not asked about where I would prefer to spend my childhood. Nobody consulted me about the kind of education I would like to receive. The friends that came into and moved out of my life never sought my permission before leaving their marks on my soul. The church my family attended, the conversations I heard, the viruses that kept me home, the weather patterns that grounded our planes, the political events that shaped our culture, the global economies that affected our savings, the college choice of the man I would marry, the personalities and genetics and health of our children—all of these things had shaped the course of my life, and yet none of it was in my hands.

What is surprising, however, is that recognizing our lack of control, rather than driving us into a tailspin of sleepless nights, drove us instead to seek God and to *rest*. I rarely in my life have slept more soundly than during those months of moving in and out of hospital rooms.

Even now I'm astonished to remember the gift of the peaceful sleep that I enjoyed in the midst of the wildly unpredictable events that swirled around us.

Being left with no choice but total dependence provided me with a very real sense of comfort because I was seeing, in countless tangible ways, that "our help comes from the Lord who made heaven and earth" (Ps. 121:2).

Who is more carefree than a small child? And yet who in the world is more helpless? I have never seen one of my toddlers pacing the playground and wringing his hands over where his next meal is going to come from. That is because a young child is not burdened with a sense of self-sufficiency or a compulsion to pull himself up by his own bootie straps. He is free to play because he knows that somebody else is watching over him and taking care of his needs. And when he rests, he sleeps (as I did) like that proverbial baby I've heard so much about.

One of the Bible passages that my husband has kept in regular circulation for many years during our morning prayer time at breakfast is Psalm 127:

> It is in vain that you rise up early
>   and go late to rest,
> eating the bread of anxious toil;
>   for he gives to his beloved sleep. (v. 2)

I mulled over these words many times after waking from yet another night of the deep and dreamless—a night spent on a plasticky hospital window seat in a room full of strange beeping and rattling. It was the kind of place I would never have been able to sleep under normal circumstances, but somehow I routinely woke to find that I had reeled in a full eight hours.

"He gives his beloved sleep." I can attest to the beautiful truth of that phrase. And, waking up to the sight of my son still breathing, I grew to love the words that followed:

> Behold, children are a heritage from the LORD,
>   the fruit of the womb a reward.
> Like arrows in the hand of a warrior
>   are the children of one's youth. (v. 3)

This son of mine was an inheritance from the Lord. It's become almost cliché to speak of our children as gifts, but clichés become clichés because they, to use another cliché, ring true. Every morning that Jonah continued to draw breath, I knew that he was a gift that might have been taken away, but that had been given back to me again. This had been true at all times, and true of all five of my children, but those intense early days of battling cancer opened my eyes to see it in a way I had never seen it before. Our days are in God's hands. Each of our days is His gift. These are clichés worth shouting from the rooftops.

Have you ever thought to thank God for the healthy production of a functional white blood cell? And another? And another? I hadn't. I recommend that you thank Him now. Every cell is His handiwork. Every inflation of your lungs is like a re-creation of Adam— the stuff of earth receiving the breath of God. Again. (Exhale.) And again.

Our lives are in God's hands, but it's not always easy to live as though we believe it. We distrust the Author and try to wrest the pen from His fingers and into our own. It's tragically laughable. Picture a preschooler trying to write a novel—and using the trunk of a giant redwood for a writing implement. This cannot end well.

If our lives are ultimately in our own hands, we must lie awake, willing lungs to fill, willing cells to divide, willing another day to come. If we alone control our destinies, then we can never rest, never turn our backs, never loosen our white-knuckle grip for a moment. But if all our moments are ultimately in our Father's hands, then we are free, like a child, to keep our own hands open— both to give and to receive a thousand other joys.

As we dealt with Jonah's cancer, our helplessness deepened our dependence on God. And dependence on God, paradoxically, brought a kind of independence—a sweet freedom from both the cares and worries that can so easily drag us toward despair and from the reckless self-reliance that can land us (smack) flat on our backs, flailing once again.

CHAPTER 8

Giving Thanks for the Fleas

Driving the ninety miles to and from the children's hospital in Spokane, Washington, on a regular basis gave me time to contemplate the landscape along our commute during all seasons of the year. We drove it in sunshine, we drove it in snow, we drove it in fog, and we drove it through sheets of relentless rain. Having grown up in the Palouse region, I knew the major landmarks well enough to anticipate what I'd see around each curve in the highway. It's a drive that has always been familiar. But at the same time, I'd never carefully *looked* at this place—at least not in the same way that I began to *really* look during those long, sometimes lonely hours on the road to Jonah's oncology appointments. Sometime during those drives, I came to realize that the views along this stretch of winding highway are as unique and lovely as any on earth.

Instead of dreading the hours stuck inside the car, and instead of anticipating the hours of waiting and needles and nausea that Jonah would soon endure, I started to look forward to simply taking in every detail of the scenery—the undulating, oceanlike beauty of our hills; the battered barns tossed like creaking ships among waves of wheat; little stands of trees huddled together like timid children dipping their feet into chilly surf; clustered lilacs, the only visible remains of farmhouses long since gone, floating like islands of purple foam in a green sea.

One brutally early morning, while the sky was still dark, Jonah and I drove west out of our sleeping Idaho town as blinking traffic lights signaled us through abandoned intersections. And as we rose up out of the valley of the next town across the Washington border, the sun suddenly slashed through a bank of low clouds above the horizon in my rearview mirror, sending a shaft of otherworldly red light across layer upon layer of velvet green hills, setting the top of each one on fire. My heart seemed to catch fire with them. It was like a painting of Pentecost, each hill a head, and on each head a tongue of flame.

No photograph could possibly do it justice. To put into pixels what these scenes put into my soul is probably impossible, but many, many times I have tried. I started to carry my camera along on these drives in an attempt to distill the sublime into pixels. In fact, a love of this place led to a side business in landscape photography—nearly all of which was shot at sixty miles per hour out the passenger side (and, I confess, sometimes out the driver side) window. But the edges of the frame always seem to do violence to the experience: like taking a knife to a canvas and cutting out the center of a masterpiece. The limits of my poor lens can never improve upon the reality lived. But how else can I share this moment that I dare not keep to myself? How can I make you understand, in some small way, what I've witnessed?

That morning, with the hills all in flame, I simply wanted to cry. Or pull the car onto the side of the road and fall to my knees in thanks. Of all the places in the world that God could have planted us during a time like this, He planted us *here*. And on those mornings, when my heart seemed like it might break for my son—or for myself—I passed through these fields, and, instead, He broke my heart with beauty.

There was a time when I wanted to leave my little north Idaho town and go somewhere more sophisticated, more urbane. I was too ambitious, too cool, too cultured, too well traveled to love this place. But as my loves matured,

I discovered, to my surprise, that really I had been too blind, too narrow, too shallow, too self-absorbed to love this place. I wasn't too big for a town this small; my heart was too small for a gift this big. Discontentment, it turns out, isn't a place you can leave behind; it's a leech that travels with you. But there is only one thing to do with a leech: kill it. And replace it with gratitude.

Through this fiery trial with cancer, God filled me with gratitude for, of all things, the rural landscape. He opened my eyes to details and subtleties that I had previously overlooked in my blind routine, and He made me long to share those glorious details with my boys, my husband, my friends, and everyone. I wanted them to see what I was finally seeing and to love it as I had grown to love it.

Father Capon was right: "A man can do worse than to be poor. He can miss altogether the sight of the greatness of small things."[10] These sunrises over farmland, these collapsing old barns, these heads of wheat turning to gold in the July sun—these are small things, I suppose. But I must not miss the greatness in them.

If there's one thing that a period of testing can do for us, it's to make us feel the weight of glory in all the things we had once brushed off so lightly. When the earth seems to be giving way beneath us, the simple

---

10 Robert Farrar Capon, *Supper of the Lamb: A Culinary Reflection* (Garden City, New York: Doubleday & Company, Inc., 1969), 25.

comfort of solid ground is a sensation we will likely never take for granted again.

Even the most mundane bits of creation contain enough divine magic to make our jaws drop simply for the mere fact that they *are*. And, as if their merely *being* isn't enough to stagger the mind, then think about *what* they are. From wet grass to whirling galaxies, from subatomic particles to glowing supergiants, we are surrounded with reasons to go positively weak-kneed with gratitude. I'm reminded of a passage in Annie Dillard's *Pilgrim at Tinker Creek* in which she sits on the ground thinking of the life teeming just beneath her and remembers: "In the top inch of forest soil, biologists found 'an average of 1,356 living creatures present in each square foot . . . Had an estimate also been made of the microscopic population, it might have ranged up to two billion bacteria and many millions of fungi, protozoa and algae—in a mere *teaspoonful* of soil.'"[11]

Every square inch—every teaspoon of dirt—contains a dance of electrons clasping their magnetic hands to form molecules that band together into cells. These cells then double and treble their numbers, transforming from seeds into roots, trunks, and leaves. The leaves unfurl in season upon the fractal patterns of branching oaks. The oaks convene in mighty forests that spread across swaths of this spinning globe. This globe, with her sister and

11 Annie Dillard, *Pilgrim at Tinker Creek* (New York: Bantam Books, 1975), 96.

brothers in their orbits, mimics the dance of electrons around the nucleus-sun, which burns in the bent arm of a galaxy that pirouettes across heaven's bright stage—with a million others—to a music that plays through millennia, and which can still be heard by those who have ears to hear it. Can you hear it? And yet these wonders, for all their splendor, are not the crowning works of God's creation. That claim belongs to you and to me and to the toddler with the runny nose and the oatmeal in his hair. Yes, him. A little lower than the angels and crowned with glory and honor.

I forget it sometimes. What are we, that God is mindful of us?[12] When circumstances get difficult, it can be easy to think that all of these happenings are beyond the scope of God's care and to lose sight of even the most obvious blessings. But when I'm tempted to start griping, the best—and perhaps the only—way to keep from slowly transforming into a bipedal Eeyore is to start looking around franticly for reasons to be thankful, and then to name them back to God. Gratitude is the best cure for gripe.

I know this doesn't come as news to anyone reading this. But knowing the importance of gratitude doesn't necessarily mean we act on it when we should—which is always. As the Apostle Paul says, "In everything give thanks; for this is the will of God in Christ Jesus for you" (1 Thess. 5:18, NKJV). During hard circumstances, it can

12 See Psalm 8:4–5 and Hebrews 2:7.

seem impossible—and even stupid—to give thanks. But once I determine to start, I rarely have to look very hard or very long. One glance at the five fingers on my hand or the solid roof over my head, and I'm off to a good start.

On several occasions when my situation has seemed particularly devoid of reasons to be grateful, this passage from a book called *The Hiding Place* creeps into my consciousness and smacks me right between the eyebrows. In it, two Dutch sisters, Corrie (the author) and Betsie ten Boom, are imprisoned in a Nazi concentration camp and are wondering what the best answer is to their latest difficulty—an infestation of fleas in their bunk house:

> "That's it, Corrie! That's [God's] answer. 'Give thanks in all circumstances!' That's what we can do. We can start right now to thank God for every single thing about this new barracks!" I stared at her; then around me at the dark, foul-aired room.
>
> "Such as?" I said.
>
> "Such as being assigned here together."
>
> I bit my lip. "Oh yes, Lord Jesus!"
>
> "Such as what you're holding in your hands." I looked down at the Bible.
>
> "Yes! Thank You, dear Lord, that there was no inspection when we entered here! Thank You for all these women, here in this room, who will meet You in these pages."
>
> "Yes," said Betsie, "Thank You for the very crowding here. Since we're packed so close, that

many more will hear!" She looked at me expectantly. "Corrie!" she prodded.

"Oh, all right. Thank You for the jammed,
crammed, stuffed, packed suffocating crowds."

"Thank You," Betsie went on serenely, "for the
fleas and for—"

The fleas! This was too much. "Betsie, there's no
way even God can make me grateful for a flea."

"Give thanks in all circumstances," she quoted.
"It doesn't say, 'in pleasant circumstances.' Fleas are
part of this place where God has put us."

And so we stood between tiers of bunks and
gave thanks for fleas. But this time I was sure Betsie
was wrong.[13]

Seriously? There they are—starved, miserable, and
trapped in some of the worst living conditions imaginable—and yet they start giving thanks? For the *fleas*? Now
that, folks, is just plain Bible-weirdo crazy.

Sometimes Betsie is the kind of pious church girl that
could drive any normal person nuts. She certainly drove
her sister Corrie nuts at times. And, in all honesty, I'm
not entirely sure whether the Bible passage they were
reading means that we must give thanks for the fleas or
to give thanks in the midst of the fleas—or even in spite
of the fleas. But in any case, they give thanks *for* the fleas.
And, as they later learn, the only reason that they had

13 Corrie ten Boom with Elizabeth and John Sherrill, *The Hiding Place*,
(Grand Rapids: Chosen, 2006), 210.

been left alone and been allowed to talk openly with the other women in their barracks was that their merciless guards refused to enter their flea-infested quarters. The *fleas* had been the reason for their only moments of freedom to develop friendships and practice their faith.

So, well, thank God for the fleas. We've all got 'em, in some form or other. And it should not surprise us to learn that God has been using even them for our ultimate good.

IN OUR DIREST CIRCUMSTANCES—EVEN WHEN you're a ten-year-old with cancer—there is always something to be thankful for. During that first year of Jonah's treatment, he was scheduled to spend Thanksgiving week in the hospital to begin a new two-month phase of chemotherapy infusions for leukemia. But early that week, his white blood cell counts were still too low for him to safely receive his chemo, so the oncologist sent him back home. Yes, home. Ordinarily this would have been a disappointing setback, delaying the end of his treatment for just that much longer. But when the setback meant staying home with his brothers all week while they were on Thanksgiving break, we were more than grateful for the delay. Three cheers for untimely immunosuppression! That week, we were grateful for a low neutrophil count that gave us a few sweet days of normal routine. We were, in a way, thanking God for fleas.

During those tumultuous months, I could hardly have expressed how inviting the phrase "normal routine" sounded. About two years before Jonah was diagnosed with cancer, I wrote an essay called "The Glorious Status Quo" in which I was, ironically, rejoicing in the discovery that I didn't have cancer. I was delighting in the news that, after discovering a suspicious lump and having a biopsy, the results came back benign, and normal life could go on as planned. Even then, I was learning to recognize the joy of being allowed to live a common, unremarkable sort of life. But after living through Jonah's battle? Nothing in the world is sweeter than a boring ol' month of school projects and basketball games and meals at home together.

And Jonah now knows, better than any teenager I've met, that just to fall asleep in your own bed each night is a gift without parallel. At age ten, he was given more than enough opportunity to recognize that there is glory in the little things—because for him the "little" things were anything but.

When was the last time you thanked God for the privilege of setting foot in a grocery store or a classroom or a church without concern that a common cold might land you in the hospital? When have you ever thought to be grateful for the simple fact that you have an appetite? For blood cells that function properly? For seeing your messy, noisy family every day at breakfast?

Pay attention to who and what is around you. These are gifts. Just a few weeks into Jonah's treatment, far from home and the rest of my family, I made a quick run to the grocery store. As I was loading the bags into my car in the Fred Meyer parking lot, I noticed something moving out of the corner of my eye. I looked up to see a bright bird of paradise, with feathers of blue and green and gold, hopping around inside the weathered cab of the dilapidated yellow pickup truck next to me. Sometimes grace is like that: beautiful and surprising—and all the more so because we find it wrapped in the most unappealing packages.

Your sorry little town? Your sterile room in the hospital? Your messy family? Your cancer? Your lonely drives through open fields? That teaspoon of dirt beneath your shoe? What can you find there? Who holds it all in His beneficent hands? Open your eyes. "The world is charged with the grandeur of God."[14] Take the time to notice, and you will always, always have cause to be grateful—even, and perhaps especially, for the fleas.

---

14 Gerard Manley Hopkins, "God's Grandeur" in *God's Grandeur and Other Poems* (New York: Dover Publications, Inc., 1995), 15.

CHAPTER 9

Mongering Fear

This past spring, on Good Friday—that day of torture and murder that we call *good*—my sons and I sat at lunch talking about this moment in the Christian calendar. One of my boys wanted answers: "So, God had already *planned* what Judas did to Jesus, right? Jesus *knew* that it was going to happen because it was part of the whole plan to save the world, right? OK, then why did Judas get blamed for it, if he was only doing what God had *planned*!?" My son was upset and confused. It's a great question. Many, many Christians wonder the same thing: If God really has planned all the details of history—if He is writing even the minor plot points in our own

91

stories—why should we bother doing anything at all? Why undergo cancer treatments, for example, if God has already established, since the foundations of the world, the exact day and time and manner of our death? How can we possibly take credit or blame for anything? If God is sovereign, why are we held responsible to act?

It's a question that generations of believers have grappled with. It chafes against our sense of individual freedom. It defies our tidy, mathematically precise categories, too. We think this must be a zero-sum game: Either God calls the shots, or we do. (Or, in God's absence, blind, impersonal natural forces do.) *Either-or.* Anything else seems contradictory. How can I be responsible for my actions if everything I do is just a line in a story being written for me by somebody else?

I'm not a professional theologian, and even if I were, I could not begin to fully answer these questions, especially in one short chapter. But at the same time, this is a matter that is foundational to how we understand our role in the cosmos and to how we live our lives in a fallen world. It's something that deserves serious consideration. So, I will offer the answer that I gave to my sons—that one of the paradoxes of our faith is that God has sovereignly ordained whatsoever comes to pass,[15] *and* that we are fully, freely responsible for our actions. "Pharaoh hardened his heart" (Exod. 8:32) and bore the consequences.

15 *Westminster Shorter Catechism*, question 7.

"The LORD hardened Pharaoh's heart" (Exod. 9:12) and accomplished His purposes.[16] *Both-and.* Do I pretend to understand how, precisely, we remain responsible for our actions while God remains the author of our lives? No. But do I believe it? Yes. I could hardly get through an average day if I didn't.

To illustrate, at age eighteen, my husband moved to L.A. to start a life of independence and rock-and-roll. Not long after arriving, he fell into a heated argument with his roommate and quickly began looking for a new place to live. If he had not had that argument, he would not have checked the classified ads for a new living situation. And if he had not checked the classifieds, then he would not have found the place to rent that he did. And if he had not found that place to rent, he would not have ended up living with a Mexican-American long-haul-truck driver named Freddie. And without witnessing Freddie's joyful Christian life, my husband might never have taken interest in going to church again. And without going to Freddie's church, he would never have met the friends who eventually led him to look deeper into theology. And without their prompting to explore deeper theology, he might never

16 If you find that paradox hard to swallow, Paul the apostle already anticipated your objection: "You will say to me then, 'Why does he still find fault? For who can resist his will?'" (Rom 9:19). Yep. That's the real question. Whaddaya say to *that*, Paul? Well, rather than delivering a satisfying three-point sermon explaining the logical ins and outs of human free will under a sovereign God, Paul shoots back with a (rather unsympathetic) retort: "Who are you, O man, to answer back to God?" Shut up and believe, in other words.

have sought out a different church. And if he had never started attending that new church, he would not have met the people who started talking to him about college as a Christian pursuit. And without that encouragement to attend college, he might never have decided to pursue a bachelor's in Idaho. And if he hadn't gone to college in Idaho, he would never have met me. And if hadn't met me, then our five young boys would never have been born. And without them, who knows what momentous future events will never happen?

So, peeling back all those layers of the narrative, do my boys owe their lives to a petty fight between a couple of immature bachelors in a Los Angeles apartment? In a word, *yes*. Or, more accurately, my boys owe their lives to the Author who wrote that inauspicious moment as the preamble to their story. But this train of events is not at all unique in its strange twists and unexpected turns. This is the story of all of us.

This is also where the problem of unfettered free will seems to me most obvious. The number of life circumstances over which we have direct control is so infinitesimal as to be almost not worth mentioning. Yes, we've made a million little choices all along the way, but the events that affected my life the most had *nothing* to do with my choices. When my parents began praying for my future spouse, years and years before I met him, this chain of events was already in the works, completely outside of my knowledge, and even further outside the scope of my personal decisions. Who planned that this particular group of guys would need a new roommate at the exact moment in history when my husband went looking? How many generations of lives hung in the balance that day? My sons' lives, certainly—and the lives of my sons' children, and their children, and so on to a thousand generations.

We all might as well be sitting with Humphrey Bogart at that bar in Morocco and marveling, "Of all the gin joints in all the towns in all the world, she walks into mine." Every moment is that *Casablanca* moment. Every one of us needs only to pull lightly on the thread of our lives that becomes the thread of our parents' lives, that becomes the thread our grandparents' lives, to discover that the fabric was formed of stitch after perfectly placed stitch, each one a *sine qua non* of our existence—a chance meeting, a missed train, or a road not taken that has, indeed, made all the difference. It's enough to make a person fall prostrate—either in despair over the utter lack of control we have over our own fates or in worship before the Author who holds every spinning atom and every passing moment in His hands.

In the words of the Westminster Shorter Catechism, "The decrees of God are, his eternal purpose, according to the counsel of his will, whereby, for his own glory, he hath foreordained whatsoever comes to pass" (question

7). *That's* what I believe. And yet, I believe we remain responsible for our actions—actions that He always uses to accomplish His purposes—at the same time. Prayer, incidentally, is one of those actions.

ONE MORNING LAST WINTER, I WAS PEERING out my kitchen window through the rain and noticed that, across the valley sloping down from my back door, a tall and barren birch was filled with dozens—maybe hundreds—of Bohemian waxwings. These birds appeared in that same tree several times over the winter months, but always at such a distance that I'd never been able to see more than their tiny silhouettes. I watched them, thinking, "I've heard that they're lovely. If only I could get a closer look!" And then, after a pause, I thought, "Why not pray for them to come nearer?"

Why not pray? I think we answer that question with a variety of excuses: *It's too small a thing. God doesn't care about things we want; He only cares about things we need. I'm not important enough for Him to listen. It's a request that doesn't matter.* Or maybe, *God simply can't be bothered.*

But the thing is, He tells us to bother Him. And He doesn't limit us to the big-ticket items: spouse, children, salvation, birth, and death. He says to pray "at all times, with every kind of prayer and petition" (Eph. 6:18, BSB). Every kind. The big and the small. All the time. He doesn't promise to say *yes* to all of our requests right away, but even the *nos* and the *not-yets* are far better answers than the passive drifting that we so frequently fall into, thinking that God doesn't traffic in the little things.

But He does. After all, He made the little things. And He delights to hear us.

So I prayed—just a quick prayer that a few of those birds would fly down closer and allow me to see them. After thirty years of living in this town and having never seen a waxwing up close, it seemed statistically unlikely that these birds would change their habits now. But oddly enough, God doesn't appear to be limited by statistical probabilities.

Moments later, I turned back toward my window, and there in the mountain ash tree next to our deck, not ten feet away from me, were scores of Bohemian waxwings, their heads crested with gold and their wings tipped with brilliant red and yellow feathers. They were more beautiful in person than I could have imagined. My boys clustered against the glass to watch with me. For a full quarter of an hour, that flock of waxwings stayed and feasted on last fall's red berries, and then at a sudden whisper from . . . Whom? . . . they took flight all at once and have not returned again. What a small and insignificant thing in the grander scheme of life. But what glory! God had answered my request with a brilliant *yes*. And all I'd done was ask.

Shouldn't we expect this? As Jesus Himself said, "Look at the birds of the air: they neither sow nor reap nor gather

9898

9898

98989898

into barns, and yet your heavenly Father feeds them. Are you not of more value than they?" (Matt. 6:26). And yet, so often, we are too afraid or too forgetful to ask.

Jesus also said that our Father even knows how many hairs end up stuck in my comb as I get ready for the day (Luke 12:7). And I'm pretty sure that, in saying so, His point wasn't to inform us that God only sweats the small stuff but leaves the bigger issues up to us. Quite the reverse. If God bothers about details so trivial to our existence that even we don't pay attention, how much *more* attention does He give to the greater concerns of our lives? He's the one who takes care of little, insignificant birds and dresses up the wildflowers—the ones we're too busy to notice, in fields where nobody sees—with splendor that outshines royalty. Do we think a God like that will somehow overlook the deepest needs of His beloved children? Hardly. He knows the day of our birth and has already plotted the moment and means of our death, and all the days in between.

So when Jonah was diagnosed with cancer, it meant going about the business of battling those malignant cells, while knowing full well that the battle, from the very beginning, belonged to the Lord.

PREPARING TO FIGHT A SERIOUS ILLNESS, cancer or otherwise, means arming yourself with great piles of technical information. This is true not only for the very vigilant, inquisitive researchers among us, but for all of us who are simply trying to navigate this strange new territory that we've landed in against our wills.

Nobody *wants* to walk into the doctor's office with an alarmingly sick child and to walk out—if you're allowed to walk out at all—with all your plans shattered and your life flipped on its head. But once this is where you are, this is where you must learn to live.

In addition to praying without ceasing, one of the things this new way of life requires is reading. A lot. The day after Jonah was diagnosed with leukemia, the hospital staff handed us a dozen different trifold brochures outlining nearly every angle of life with cancer: Housing options. Helping siblings cope. Dealing with financial stress. Navigating marital tensions. Keeping up in school. Managing side effects. Facing fear of death. We also received whole books and binders full of information on the details of the medical treatment itself, as well as blank notebooks designed specifically for taking notes of our own.

In a few short weeks, we had perused and begun to memorize a long list of unpronounceable, polysyllabic terms: names of chemotherapy, steroid, and antiemetic drugs, as well as names of the various types and subtypes of leukemia, not to mention other forms of pediatric cancer that we encountered daily in the hospital. We read up on risks, side effects, treatment schedules, survival

statistics, and more. We read about the history of leukemia treatment and about experimental therapies involv-
ing genetically modified T-cells and viruses. We skimmed
through websites and pamphlets and health magazines.

We also encountered plenty of alternative articles and
anecdotes (some of them sad, some of them intriguing,
and some of them hilarious) about people who had cast
off the standard medical treatment and claimed to have
found ways to cure cancer through juice diets, organic
veganism, ingesting baking soda, eliminating sugar, eating the ground up pits and seeds of fruit, and even inject-
ing themselves with their own urine.

Friends and family, especially early on in Jonah's
treatment, loved to share suggestions and links and news
clippings about unconventional treatments or promising
new therapies. And although some of the parents I met
at the hospital took gestures of this sort as a personal
attack on their parenting decisions or on their intelli-
gence, I usually didn't mind. Usually. The surgeries, toxic
drugs, and radiation treatments these kids endure are, in
the words of one oncologist, "barbaric. But it's the best
we've got." No, I was not going to sign Jonah up for coffee ground enemas or fly him to a foreign hospital with
sketchy credentials to receive urine injections, but you
bet I was interested in learning about the more humane
options that might eventually be available to leukemia
patients like our son.

While cancer research is a rapidly changing field, and while plenty of the news coming out of that research is both fascinating and encouraging, forty years ago, our son would most likely have been dead in a matter of weeks. Today he has roughly a ninety percent chance of remaining leukemia free for life. The statistics are steadily moving in the right direction, and I am deeply grateful. But statistics are only a small part of Jonah's story, and they are certainly not the foundation of our hope for his life.

Sorting through the statistics and "breaking news" reports and "shocking" exposés is dizzying business. Even as a Christian, it's easy to be swayed one direction and then another by every health article under the sun. We want to think that if we eat the right foods or avoid the wrong substances, we'll be immune to all kinds of physical suffering—especially cancer. Believing that we can escape suffering by just doing the right things makes us feel safe. And the reason it feels safe is because it seems to put us back in control. This, in turn, can also give us a sense of superiority over those whose health is failing. "Well," we think smugly, "too bad they're sick, but they must have done something to bring this on themselves." In a way, we're not all that different from Job's so-called friends, insisting that his suffering must have been punishment for something he'd done to offend God. Or we're like Jesus' disciples wondering, "Who sinned, this man or his parents, that he was born blind?" (John 9:2).

The only difference is that, in the modern world, we don't believe that the suffering comes from offending the God of heaven; it comes from offending the fickle gods of health. Our modern version might read, "Who consumed too many pesticides (breathed too much smog, absorbed too much chlorine, ate too much sugar), this man or his parents, that he was diagnosed with cancer?" We point the accusing finger because we like to comfort ourselves with the thought that by following the ten-thousand commandments of health, no matter how often they are repealed and replaced, cancer cannot touch us.

But Jesus gives an answer that surprised His disciples and that should also surprise the disciples of health: This happened "that the works of God might be displayed in him" (John 9:3).

Say *what*, now? That doesn't fit our narrative at all.

We generally assume that entirely impersonal forces are at work through certain foods or germs or chemical reactions. And, yes, God created a world in which actions have consequences and in which cigarettes have a close connection to lung cancer. I know all that. But we must be careful; we very often have *no idea* what is going on behind the scenes when it comes to our health, and we very rarely ask what God might be up to in the suffering we see around us. Instead, we offer interpretations that imply that if we follow the current rules, it can't happen to us.

We gravitate toward any explanation that puts *us* in control. Why? Because the alternative is terrifying.

The more I've read about cancer, the more it seems that health publications (both mainstream and alternative) absolutely could not stay in business without a widespread and crippling fear of cancer. To equip ourselves with information is one thing. To petrify ourselves with information is another.

Scroll through a hundred health blogs, and flip through a teetering stack of health magazines, and it seems that the headlines stick to an endlessly repeated theme: "5 Foods that Fight Cancer." "12 Secret Weapons Against Cancer." "17 Strategies for Staying Cancer-Free." "6 Myths about Cancer." "3 Signs that You Might Have Cancer." Clearly, without the fear of cancer (and without numbered lists), readership would plummet.

For all of these publications, *fear* is what brings home the bacon. And bacon, according to the Great Oracle, the Internet, also causes leukemia.

Believe me, I fully understand the desire to learn more about what causes cancer and what cures it. Boy, do I ever. As I've already mentioned, I had a cancer scare of my own a few years ago, and I, like most people I know, have had friends and relatives who died of various forms of cancer. It's a disease that touches the lives of just about everybody, so it's no surprise that we fear it. But it's also no surprise that there are people who are eager to both prey upon and to perpetuate our fears.

I once read a post, shared by a well-meaning Facebook friend, with the headline, "Finally! Johns Hopkins Medical School Reveals the Truth about Cancer!" The link offered a list of generic tips (Stop eating refined sugars!) but also endorsed a number of supplements—by brand name—that we should buy. It was an artful combination of common sense, sheer madness, and advertising genius. This seemed more than a little fishy, so I checked the sources. It turned out, of course, to be a hoax; Johns Hopkins had shared no such thing and had devoted a whole page of its website to dispelling the misinformation and outright lies contained in that article. But by the time the article reached me, the link had already been shared on Facebook upwards of twenty thousand times.

The reason I think we are so willing to read all those cancer articles and to believe sketchy posts like the one I mentioned is that they give us a comforting illusion of control. And, if we're honest, cancer, more than almost any other disease, makes us feel very, very, *out* of control because it is still, in spite of all that up-to-date information (and misinformation), shrouded in mystery.

Why does one of our children get leukemia while the rest remain perfectly healthy? Why did one of my mom's siblings get cancer while none of the other eight have? How is it possible that a man I know who smoked his entire life never gets lung cancer, while a friend's mother, who never even smoked a single cigarette, dies of the disease? The answer, from what I can tell, is this: *We don't know*. Really, we don't. Cancer is a bogey that seems to lurk around every corner, and we feel helpless against it.

But that sense of helplessness, however much we fight it, gives us a glimpse of something like Truth. And that kind of Truth can be terrifying. Our days are numbered, and not—contrary to our hopes and wishes—by us. So it's easy, even for Christians who should know better, to want to panic in the face of our helplessness and to grasp at some semblance of control. We could easily spend every waking hour trying to keep up with the latest health advice—even when we know that the latest health advice has changed on us and will change on us again and again and again.

First, we're told to hide from the sun to avoid cancer. And then we find out that our sun boycott is causing Vitamin D deficiency, which can cause cancer. So we start chugging fish oil for the Vitamin D. But then we are told that the fish oil can be tainted with mercury, which is linked to cancer. We work hard to provide our families with good nutrition that will fight cancer. But then it turns out that kids who have better nutrition are also more likely to be tall, which apparently puts them at greater risk for cancer. And then when we finally do get cancer, we fight it with radiation and toxic drugs—both of which can cause cancer.

Cancer, like Shakespeare's fool Touchstone, chases us
around the world-stage, shouting, "I will kill thee a hundred and fifty ways!"[17]

I don't think it's simply a fool's errand to try to steer
clear of this threat to our health, especially not after all
that we've been through with Jonah. But at the same
time, there does come a point when concern for health
becomes obsession with health—when prudence crosses
the line into panic, and we lose sight of God's promises
and providence.

As I've read the Bible during the years since Jonah's
diagnosis, I've noticed that God (you know—the One
who made our bodies in the first place?) makes an aston-
ishing number of promises related to health and strength
and long life. And yet I haven't come across a single one
of those promises that hinges on nutrition or exercise or
any of the usual concerns.

I still believe that those concerns are the means that
God routinely uses to sustain our lives. I, too, have been
known to take my vitamins, eat my greens, and warn my
kids about the dangers of cigarettes. But if I were trying to
compile a list of "Biblical Tips for Better Health," I think
it would have a whole lot less to do with consuming organic produce and joining the gym, and a whole lot more
to do with fearing God (Deut. 6:24), honoring parents

17 William Shakespeare, *As You Like It*, Cynthia Marshall, ed., (Cambridge: Cambridge University Press, 2004), V.1.49.

(Exod. 20:12, Prov. 4:20–22), befriending Lady Wisdom (Prov. 3:16; 4:7–10), and seeking first the Kingdom of God and His righteousness (Luke 12:22–34).

Not a hair can fall from our heads (Matt. 10:29–31)—or a cancer cell form in our bodies—without the will of our Father in heaven. He knows what we need before we ask, which means I don't have to keep tying myself into awkward knots in my attempts to keep up with all the latest cancer-dodging advice. Resting in God's care allows me to take a step back from the fears of the moment and to gain some perspective on this salutary game of Twister—and to laugh a little. And a joyful heart, after all, "is good medicine" (Prov. 17:22).

Ultimately, our lives are not in our hands. And that truth, instead of scaring us, should allow us to loosen our kung-fu death grip on health, to step away from all those hot-off-the-presses articles about the latest cancer scare, and to *quit worrying*. Seriously. Quit. Worrying is bad for our health. Even the latest medical research concurs.[18] And which of us by worrying can add a single day to his life (Luke 12:25)? Rather, "Fear the Lord and depart from evil. It will be health to your flesh and marrow to your bones" (Prov. 3:7b-8).

Marrow to your bones. Now *there's* a verse to which any leukemia patient might cling.

---

18 "Sick with Worry: How Thoughts Affect Your Health," https://www.agingcare.com/articles/health-problems-caused-by-stress-143376.htm.

CHAPTER 10

I Grow Old, I Grow Old

I n the early days of Jonah's treatment, I parked in the children's hospital garage next to an SUV that had the words "CHILDHOOD CANCER SUCKS!" scrawled in gold paint across the back windows. I might not put it in exactly those terms, but I don't disagree.

I have spent long, sleepless nights in a windowless emergency room, the backs of my legs sticking to my vinyl seat cushion, while my child's cries of pain come in successive waves, muffled by the surgical mask he wears and by the hum of the IV pump dripping morphine through a needle in his chest. I have lain awake in the dark, keeping vigil to a symphony of suffering: the frantic beat of helicopter blades outside our window, the rhythmic beep of heart monitors and IVs, the treble whisper of night nurses, the soprano wail of small children, and a percussive cough keeping time behind a closed door down the hall. I have spent exhausted days watching my young son vomit for hours, while his hair falls out and his wide eyes plead for a relief that is far from coming. We have waged war against anger, fear, worry, loneliness, discouragement, and pain. I have wept for son. I have wept for his brothers. I have wept for my husband. I have wept for myself.

Childhood cancer sucks.

But, for the record, you need to know that cancer is not the worst thing that can happen to you. Not even close. In fact, we have gained so much from this experience that we are now able to look back and see that cancer was actually one of the *best* things that ever happened to us. I don't say the *easiest*; the best things never are. We have all certainly grown and matured spiritually as a direct result of the conversations and experiences that cancer brought us. But cancer has also given us many other little reasons to be grateful. Even during the hardest stages of his treatment, Jonah discovered that a life-threatening illness is not without its perks.

Thanks to his leukemia, our baseball-loving firstborn was invited to throw the first pitch at a Spokane Indians game, escorted onto the field by Super Bowl MVP Mark Rypien. Jonah was also asked to the throw out the first pitch at a College World Series game. He has been inside the dugout and on the field to shake hands with Seattle Mariners. He's had movie star Joel Courtney come spend an afternoon with him flying paper airplanes off a second-story balcony. A small mountain of books and toys and crafts and cards and even an iPad were given to him, thanks to the kindness of those who heard of his plight. And, as a cherry on top of the icing on the cake, the Make-A-Wish foundation sent our entire family on an all-expenses-paid vacation to Hawaii, where our boys surfed for the first time, snorkeled with tropical fish, took a private tour of the USS Missouri at Pearl Harbor, and swam with dolphins. After seeing all of the privileges and gifts poured out on Jonah, one of our other boys once said, "Aw, man! I wish *I* had cancer." And the wish was entirely understandable.

The children's hospital, in spite of all the hard memories associated with its rooms, has also become a place that my boys love to visit. The staff and volunteers there have worked so hard to create a welcoming environment for these sick kids that all our boys clamor for the chance to go along with Jonah for his checkups. Jonah himself sometimes laments that his days of staying overnight at the hospital are over. He grew to love the nurses we met, and he basked in all the one-on-one attention from parents and grandparents. His memories of cancer are so well seasoned with blessings that he has more than once told us that he wishes he could start his treatment all over again. And he is no masochist. This was simply the best-worst time of his life.

A SECOND BENEFIT OF JONAH'S CANCER WAS

that it forced us to begin the kinds of conversations that so many people prefer to put off for decades, if not forever. Our ten-year-old knew that having cancer meant death was a real possibility for him. We needed to talk about dying. He *wanted* us to talk about dying. And so we did.

We had known our fair share of older Christians who had died, and we had talked about their deaths with joyful sadness, knowing that these longsuffering believers were now freed from pain and present with the Lord. But for us, death had always seemed like a distant threat—an event that we could discuss comfortably because it happened to other people. Older people. Weaker people. *Sicker* people.

Not anymore. My five fidgety boys, my husband, and I sat around the kitchen table one afternoon, with the sun pouring through the large double-paned window, and we talked about death. This may sound morbid, but to be given an opportunity to talk about this uncomfortable topic so openly meant that we could also talk about what waits for us beyond it. Donne was right: "one short sleep past, we wake eternally, and death shall be no more." Death shall die.[19]

19 John Donne, Holy Sonnet X: "Death Be Not Proud" (1609).

That night, as I tucked him into bed, Jonah kept returning to our discussion. *What will heaven be like?* I told him what little I could. *And what about the resurrection? What will it be like to have a body that can never die?* Together we imagined what places we might explore with eternity before us, what musical instruments we might take up. *Who will be there? What people we will meet in the flesh?* Bach, his musical hero! Our great grandparents! Moses! Paul! The original Jonah! Jesus Himself! This was not abstract theology for him; it was personal.

Jonah went to sleep that night with a smile on his face, almost excited about the prospect of passing through death to that life on the other side. This experience was a gift. It was one I needed as much as he did. I never expected that I would be required to have these conversations with children so young, but I am grateful.

Death has not ceased to be the enemy. It is still a curse. It still does violence to the union of body and soul. And I would be lying to say that none of us has ever feared death since that day. But we live on this side of Easter, and Death has lost its sting. As our pastor said in a recent sermon, Jesus passed into the grave before us and came through on the other side and is calling to us, "Come on! Don't be afraid! It's safe!" Death, for the Christian, is safe. Our Savior descended through the grave to Death's door, bursting it open, breaking the lock that would have held us all, and took away the keys. That is why, sitting cross-legged on the bed with my pale, cancer-ravaged boy, we were able to look the Last Enemy squarely in the face—and *laugh*.

I pray that this same laughter will be on our lips well into silvery old age.

FOR MANY YEARS NOW, MY HUSBAND HAS made a point of taking our family to a local nursing home to bring a little joy to the lonely and afflicted. We wander through the dining room, greeting some of the aging residents we've met on previous visits, many of whom are happy to meet us again for the first time—every time. After one of these visits, my five-year-old, Asaph, said to me, "Mom? You know that place where people go to live until they die?" I nodded, knowing exactly what place he meant. "Well, I saw an old lady there who was sitting in a wheelchair, and her *teeth* were out, so she pushed them back into her mouth! I said hi to her, but she didn't hear me."

It's shocking, isn't it, son? It's shocking that we crumble until our legs cannot hold us. Until our teeth fall out of our mouths. Until our ears grow numb to the voices of children hollering "Hi!" six inches from our heads. But what's more shocking is that we, with our smooth skin and strong limbs, forget this about ourselves.

Here in this university town of ours, where the beautiful and the invincible spill out of every coffee shop and swarm the sidewalks and shopping malls, we find that the fresh supply of youth never dries up. We spend our days in the houses of feasting, toasting each other's health, and checking out each other's sexy curves. Meanwhile, life's epilogue is lived out behind closed doors, along sterile hallways under fluorescent lights, so that the rest of us can forget the final pages of our story.

But not my children. My own Jonah has slept within the black innards of the whale. He has looked death straight in the mouth and smelled its foul breath. My own little blue-eyed five-year-old has navigated those urine-scented hallways in the house of mourning and learned some wisdom (Eccles. 7:2–4). He has seen our latter end.

We can fight against it, and we can pretend to believe otherwise, but the truth is that we are all in that place where we will live until we die. I will certainly try to push that final day back as long as I reasonably can, but I never want to spend so much time simply staying alive that I forget to *live*.

EIGHT YEARS AGO, WHEN MY PATERNAL grandmother—the one who spent much of her life worrying—fell and ended up in the hospital, none of us anticipated a prolonged recovery. She had hit her head, and she was weakened by the injury, but the bruise would heal, and she would quickly be well again. She had always gotten well again. Hers had already been a long life.

But a life, to be called "long," must have an end; eternity is not a span that can be measured in lengths, and so it seemed that this long life of hers must have an end, as well. Watching her move painfully in her bed while she rested from her injuries in the nursing home, I could see that her winter had come. In spite of a brief Indian summer, the first frost had already taken its toll. She complained of the chill in the air, and her limbs were more frail, her hands less steady.

I see her gnarled fingers and papery skin in my mind's eye still, and the image sometimes frightens me, but not because I am afraid of death. I am afraid to grow old.

She was a Christian, but as the years passed, it became clear that she was terrified to die. She refused to discuss it. She refused to read about it. She refused to accept it. In all my conversations with her, she avoided any reference to it. And right as we were in the throes of Jonah's cancer treatments, preparing him for the prospect of death, death came for her instead—but she was not prepared. As she lay dying, she was overcome not by joyful anticipation or peace or resignation, or even pain and sadness, but by a fear that bordered on panic. The last time I saw her conscious, she was racked with sobs, clinging tearfully and desperately to a life that was already gone.

Some of it may have been the medications talking. Some of it may have been the natural apprehension that even the most stalwart believers among us must feel as we prepare to step into that "undiscovered country."[20] But it unnerved me to see her so undone.

It also made me wonder: In an age when medical advances have pushed death farther and farther off for most of us, are we failing to prepare ourselves for the day it finally comes? Because it *will* come. I sometimes hear people say they want to "die well." But what do they mean? I'm afraid that by "dying well," we now simply mean dying comfortably—without pain.

Karl Marx once famously said, "Religion is the opiate of the masses,"[21] and many still agree. They regard religion as a crutch—a coping mechanism for the unenlightened. And while they may see it as delusional, the Christian religion gives its followers the hope and the courage to die without fear. How odd, then, that our culture has come full circle and now welcomes not religion but medication—namely, morphine—as that which gives us the hope and the courage to die without fear. Opiates have become the opiate of the people.

We arm ourselves with health magazines and running shoes and convince ourselves that we can be immortal.

20 Shakespeare, *Hamlet*, Act III, Scene 1.
21 John Raines, ed., *Marx on Religion* (Philadelphia: Temple University Press), 5.

And when, at last, our green smoothies and vitamins let us down and our bodies fail, we medicate our way through death.

But why? What is the point?

In all its chasing after health, the world rarely stops to ask what it's all for. What *is* the chief end of man? The health industry specializes in extending our lives but never bothers to give us the *reason* we should want to live longer. It's simply taken for granted that we should want to live for a very long time. And it's true: I do want my boys to live to be old men. And I want to live to see my grandchildren. Of course I do. Life is a good gift. But it's more than that; it's a gift with a purpose.

If I give my kid a hammer for his birthday, it's not because I want to simply make him the proud owner of a shiny, carefully wrapped hunk of metal. No, I want him to use it. I want him to build something with it. By the time he's done with it, I want to see that thing pitted with rust, worn on the edges, and bearing the scars of long years spent constructing things of value. Life is *that* kind of gift.

As one author friend put it, "Life is meant to be spent."[22] Long life can be a great blessing, but what good is a long shelf life if our contents are never used up before we reach our expiration date? Better to be a cheap

22   N.D. Wilson, *Death by Living: Life is Meant to be Spent*, (Nashville: Thomas Nelson, 2013).

plastic jug of grape juice cocktail—or a boring old cup of cold water—that is poured out to quench someone's thirst than to be a bottle of the finest Châteauneuf-du-Pape that is kept safely corked on a shelf for decade after decade until its contents turn into vinegar.

My mom's dad (who died of cancer) did not live as long as many of his peers, but he also lived *more* within those years than many of his peers. He learned to speak English, served in a war, raised nine children, was faithful to his wife, ran a dairy farm, felled trees (as well as a few of his fingers), worked in the church, owned a retirement home, excelled at bowling, and shared his home with his dozens of grandchildren.

Once, when I was about the same age that Asaph was when he saw the old woman's teeth fall out, my grandfather took me aside and whispered, "Did you know that I can whistle and brush my teeth at the same time?" I walked with him to the bathroom sink, where he popped out his dentures, picked up a toothbrush, and started whistling. I thought it was hilarious—him brushing away, holding his dentures with his good hand and the toothbrush with the mangled fingers of his other hand, while a merry tune played on his wrinkled lips. I laughed, and he laughed with me.

When death creeps nearer and my own teeth fall out, I hope it will make my little grandchildren laugh. And I hope to be laughing with them.

CHAPTER 11

Wasted Potential

S itting in Jonah's hospital room one afternoon, watching him try—and fail—to keep up with his school work, it occurred to me that, even if he were cured of cancer, my son might never be the same kid he had once been. I had always felt a great deal of personal pride in his accomplishments. This was my son in whom I was well pleased. He was a good student, a natural athlete, and a skilled pianist, but I hadn't fully realized how much those achievements meant to me until I saw how easily they could be taken away. I had been concerned for his survival, but once it seemed that he might keep his life, I grew more deeply concerned that he might lose his standing and reputation for excellence.

I had staked so much of my own confidence on his successes that I wasn't sure how I would respond to failure. I had thought I was taking loving pride in him, but I discovered that, through him, I had also been taking selfish pride in my own apparent success and skill as a parent. I had produced this amazing kid. I could take much of the credit, I thought, for who he had become. And I, while I truly was concerned for him, for his own sake, could also hardly bear to think that he might lose that edge—that success—that reflected so well on *me*.

So I tried to push him to study harder in the hospital, to practice piano on the little black keyboard the music therapist provided, to keep him busy with maintaining what skills he could. But as he fell further and further behind, and as I worried that he might have to repeat a grade or lose his competitive edge, I finally had to take a close look at my own heart. These fears for him, I realized, had sometimes been as much for my own reputation as for his own well-being. I had wanted him to live up to his incredible potential as a student, an athlete, and a musician. Instead, God had clearly wanted him to live up to a very different kind of potential—the kind for which I could take no credit at all.

LIVING UP TO OUR POTENTIAL IS, APPARENTLY, a noble and attainable goal. After all, every time an election cycle begins, politicians clog the airwaves with promises to fund initiatives that will help kids live up to their potential—or, on a grander scale, to help *America* live up to its potential, whatever that means. And if you can crawl under a rock long enough to ignore the stump speeches, a quick internet search will pull up hundreds of articles from major parenting, business, and news sources offering "The 5 Qualities of People Who Live Up to Their Potential" (mindbodygreen.com), or advice on "Maximizing Your Child's Potential" (drphil.com), or the sad reasons "Why Most People Don't Reach Their Full Potential" (forbes.com).

Every desire, we're led to believe, is within reach. I saw an interview with President Trump, just before he took office, telling a reporter that the secret to his success was to never, ever give up. Ever. Just keep doing what you love, and success will happen.

That's the "secret," is it? It's hardly an idea that's been hidden under a bushel until now. How many thousands of graduation addresses around the globe have this as their theme? How many award acceptance speeches from pop-stars-*du-jour*? How many fundraising pleas for our failing schools? How many interviews with the MVP of the big game? The same three-chord anthem is everywhere: *Follow your dreams. Never give up. Live up to your potential.* This is the magic recipe for "success." It's also the magic recipe for brewing up million-gallon vats full of bubbling self-delusion, from which short, asthmatic teenage boys drink deep and believe, in their heart of hearts, that they will someday play for the NBA.

If they fail? Well, it's probably because they stopped believing in themselves and gave up.

In many of the articles I've seen, the implication is that failing to achieve our dreams is pretty much always our fault. Maybe we didn't follow our passion. Or maybe we got carried away by our passions. We listened to the naysayers. We didn't heed the warnings of the naysayers. We didn't put in those extra hours. We put in too many extra hours and didn't lead a balanced life.

As the possibilities for the future continue to narrow with every passing year, it's all too easy to face that reality with more than a little regret and fear. *My dreams have died,* we tell ourselves. *My talents are wasted and unappreciated. I deserve so much more!*

And the world is ready and eager to dish out advice on how to get those things that we fear we may have lost: *You need to break free! Look out for number one! Make a fresh start! Cleanse your life of toxic relationships that stand between you and your goals! If you dream big, work hard, and never give up, you can succeed at anything!* Thus say the politicians, the advertisements, the self-help books, and a mega-church pastor or two. This kind of talk, I imagine, is where so many of those stories of wild mid-life crises arise.

Christians may recognize the hot air and half-truths for what they are, but we still aren't always immune to them—or to the thought that *this* surely cannot be *all* that God intended for my life. Which of us has not, if just for a moment, thought about everything we have failed to achieve and wondered whether we could have done anything—or have been anyone—more important? In every direction, we are offered up honey-sweet words of flattery tempting us toward self-delusion, self-worship, and self-pity, all of it dripping with the attractive lie that *we deserve so much more* than what God has given us.

What we deserve, however, because of our sin, is—to put it bluntly—death (Rom. 6:23). The Bible says it pretty unambiguously. Am I alive? Well, then, I deserve worse. But that just doesn't sell magazines. So we let the world, the flesh, and the devil coax us into believing that what we deserve is the royal treatment. And we are taught to expect it, to demand it, and to fear not getting it—while failing to realize that in Christ we are royalty already.

I'm not immune to this temptation. I'm not immune to thinking that my gifts are being wasted or that my identity and worth are found in the things I have or do or make. When I look back at my own education and upbringing, at my hobbies and interests, I see plenty of potential that has, by all appearances, gone to waste. There were plenty of activities in which I showed some glimmer

of promise—math, science, languages, painting, music—
and at which I thought I might have excelled. But the
truth is that I couldn't pursue them all. I chose only a few
to chase after and watched the rest slip into the rearview
mirror and then slide out of sight behind the last hill. In
becoming a wife, and then a mother, many of the things
I *had* gotten good at also had to be laid down, at least for
a time. I could not simultaneously hold both a baby and
a full-time job. I have left thousands of broken bits of
unrealized potential in my wake. Haven't we all?

And what about all those other things that we were
never even given the chance to try? We have whole reser-
voirs of unrealized potential where we never even dipped
our little toes. We could have been virtuosos on instruments that we've never touched! We and Jane Austen's
Lady Catherine de Bourgh might as well share the same
empty sentiment: "If I had ever learnt, I should have been
a great proficient."[23]

Wasted potential. That's what it is. All of it. And it's
happening to our kids, too, right under our potentially
famous noses. I have literally lain awake at night wondering if we've failed as parents by not signing our kids
up for hockey or wrestling or Boy Scouts or violin—that
these might have turned out to be the very activities in
which my boys' talents would truly have shone, if only we
had let them try.

23 Jane Austen, *Pride and Prejudice* (New York: E.P Dutton, 1906), 176.

If only. The very thought could make me laugh. Or cry. But mostly laugh.

Of course, it really is possible that our failures are due to sloth and apathy, and of that we must repent. But if my failure to learn cello is due not to laziness but to human finitude and hard work in other areas, there is no cause to mourn over wasted potential or to boast about what I imagine I could have been. And who really wants to be remembered as the Lady Catherine character in the story we've been living? The number of might-have-beens is truly infinite—and the days of our lives truly finite—which is why "potential" is such a laughably useless word when it has no object.

Potential for what? That's the question that most of those articles and books and stump speeches fail to address. None of us has lived up to his full potential for acts of violence, either, but that is hardly a reason to sigh with remorse.

In seeing Jonah's school work, piano skills, and athletic strength slipping, I finally had to recognize that God was shaping my child into something other than I had planned. Instead of learning history and science, Jonah was learning wisdom through suffering; instead of practicing Bach and Mozart, he was practicing patience in trials; instead of training for curve balls and jump shots, he was training for empathy through pain. I saw a very different kind of potential taking shape than anything I had planned for him. *These* talents, and not those others, were what God was giving him to invest and to return to Him with interest.

It was not easy to let go of my own desires (is it ever?), but with time I learned instead to love what God was doing in and through Jonah. Indeed, all of my sons were becoming a different and better kind of people through this experience, and I had to humble myself to see that this gift—this potential for grace and wisdom—had nothing whatsoever to do with me or my great parenting or my careful planning. It was all gift. Even the things for which I had been taking the credit were a gift from God. And if I had continued clinging to those things that God was clearly in the process of taking away (or putting on hold), I could not have faced my son's future with the kind of hope and joy that only He provides.

Just last winter, a few days before Christmas, Jonah slipped and fell on the ice in the doorway outside the school gym—after a full afternoon of sledding the day before and after two back-to-back basketball practices that morning—and broke his wrist. All that high-action activity without a single injury, and he ends up in the emergency room on account of walking out the door. It's kind of funny. But once again, it was an exercise in patience, learning to again lay down all the things that God had suddenly said "no" to. He had been looking forward to a very different kind of Christmas break. And now? No piano. No basketball. No snowball fights. And with school starting and him still in a cast, even the typing elective he'd signed up for seemed unlikely to go as planned.

Wasted potential? No. Seeds planted. Nothing, including our "potential," is ever wasted when it is entrusted to a God who takes even what is dead and raises it up in glory. Whatever good Jonah might have enjoyed with two good arms last Christmas, God asked him to lay it down in order to learn something better—patience and trust in place of pass-fakes and trills.

PURSUING OUR DREAMS AND LIVING UP TO our potential may sound sexy, but it is an impossible— and sometimes a dangerous—goal when isolated from all that God has called us to be.

According to a recent article in *Time*, many mothers fantasize about running away from home to pursue their ambitions.[24] I certainly know a thing or two about that. But the author of the article blames this desire on the vestiges of patriarchy, inequality, lack of childcare benefits, and so on. The implication is that if only the playing field were finally leveled with giant cultural bulldozers, that deep discontent would entirely disappear. But I humbly disagree. Hard or unfair circumstances can

24 Gayle Foreman, "Moms, Your Fantasy About Running Away Is Totally Normal," http://time.com/4483909/leave-me/.

present unique temptations, it's true, but a change in external circumstances alone can do little to clean up an envy-infected soul.

Whether I'm walking the red carpet or vacuuming the living room carpet, discontent will travel with me unless my measure of success is grounded in something deeper than fame or money or career or realized potential. We may think that happiness is found by achieving fame and fortune. But by that standard, some of the world's most "successful" people have, nevertheless, descended into despair. The pursuit of our own glory apart from the glory of the One who bestows it cannot possibly end well. Do we really think we can do better for ourselves than He will do for us when we follow Him? What does it profit us if we gain the whole world, and yet lose our souls (Mark 8:36)?

I am not saying that we should have no godly ambition. Not at all. God loves excellence, and we should pursue it. As Proverbs has it, "Do you see a man skillful in his work? He will stand before kings" (Prov. 22:29). We ought to take what our Master has given us and return it to Him with interest (Matt. 25:26–27). But ambition can be a slippery thing. Our motives are often hard to pin down, and we must remember that God's economy is one of paradox: the way to glory is the way of the cross.

The siren song of selfish ambition can be drowned out only by the kind of song found in Philippians 2—the "hymn of Christ," the *cantus Christi:*

> Do nothing from selfish ambition or conceit, but in
> humility count others more significant than your-
> selves. Let each of you look not only to his own in-
> terests, but also to the interests of others. Have this
> mind among yourselves, which is yours in Christ
> Jesus, who, though he was in the form of God, did
> not count equality with God a thing to be grasped,
> but emptied himself, by taking the form of a ser-
> vant, being born in the likeness of men. And being
> found in human form, he humbled himself by be-
> coming obedient to the point of death, even death
> on a cross. (vv. 3–8)

What is it that I should be doing "out of selfish ambition or conceit" (2:3)? Nothing. What great potential
did we set aside for the sake of our family, our neighbors,
our friends? Maybe even for our enemies? Did we empty
ourselves of "equality with God" (2:6)? No? What greater
claim could there be? Yet if God Himself did not consider it a thing to be grasped, how much more should we be
willing to let go of our petty claims to greatness?

If the Lord of glory, in whom all things hold together, would stoop to be born into poverty, to serve, to suffer, and to die for people like us, then is it possible that
I could let go of those ambitions that are getting in the
way of loving God and my neighbor? Could I "waste my
potential" for the sake of those whom I've been called
to serve?

It should go without saying, but because we are finite, and because our possibilities are infinite, we can never live up to all the potential we might have. Not in this life. But that should not fill us with fear or send us frantically chasing after our misbegotten dreams before the clock runs out. We can chuck our bucket lists into the bucket, if necessary, because we have far *more* than this life to look forward to. The story does not end when God calls us to lay down our ambitions and our claims of earthly greatness. In many ways, this is where the better story really begins.

Do we *really* want to live up to our potential for something great? Fair enough. Jesus doesn't tell us not to desire it; He tells us how to go about it: "Whoever wishes to become great among you shall be your servant; and whoever wishes to be first among you shall be slave of all. For even the Son of Man did not come to be served, but to serve, and to give His life a ransom for many" (Mark 10:43–45, NASB).

When God call us to duties and sacrifices, or trials like cancer, that turn our paths away from the goals we had set for ourselves, it's easy to fear that our gifts are simply being wasted. But are they? When we follow God's call and not our own, have we truly wasted our potential—throwing it out like trash? Or have we laid it down and planted it where our heavenly Father will raise and transform it into glorious resurrection fruit?

CHAPTER 12

Weeping with Those Who Weep

(and Guilt-Tripping Those Who Rejoice)

"Remember that little girl you used to play with at the hospital?" I asked my boys. "The one you pulled through the hallway in the red wagon? She died last week."

In our well-fed, bubble-wrapped, vitamin-popping, disinfected part of the world, this isn't the kind of news that most parents need to pass on to their children. The death of a child simply isn't a topic that gets mentioned in your average modern parenting books: "Chapter Six—Coping with the Death of a Childhood Friend."

On the one hand, I can be nothing but grateful that this kind of scenario is so rare as to be almost not worth preparing for. The death of our kids' playground buddies is not a common occurrence. But on the other hand, it's the rarity of childhood mortality that makes it so much more shocking when it does happen. This, I'm sure, has never been the kind of news that any parent in the history of the world has been fully ready to bring before their children, but it seems clear that in other times and places it was not entirely unexpected. Reading biographies of people who lived as recently as a century ago—or who live right now in war-torn or impoverished parts of the world—reveals how ruthlessly common childhood mortality can be. A mother of a dozen children might easily have expected to see only a handful grow into adulthood. Wander through the older sections of your local graveyard, and you can probably find plots where child after child from the same family is memorialized by tiny headstones. Rachel weeping for her lost children is a sound that has echoed through centuries.

Even now, I have many friends and relatives whose little ones have died in the womb. But for moms like me who live in the relative safety, peace, and comfort of the contemporary, industrialized world, the death of an older child is almost beyond comprehension. It's a mercifully—but devastatingly—uncommon event, which means that most of us are utterly unprepared when it confronts us. And we are equally unprepared for how to tell our children, "*A child you know has died.*"

After spending so much time in hospitals, around other kids with life-threatening diseases, however, this is something I have had to tell my kids on more than one occasion. And it is never easy.

I wish I could say that breaking the news to my boys is hard because it causes my children sorrow. But that's not the case. In my experience, kids respond to the news of most deaths—except for those of their very closest friends and family—with almost the same degree of sadness that they express after learning that the Mariners lost to the Twins: a brief look of surprise and disappointment, followed by cries of, "Really? Whoa. Too bad!" Then, after a brief pause, questions about what's for lunch. That's it.

The older boys will probably want to know more details about how it happened and when, and their troubled expressions of surprise will last a few moments longer. But very rarely have I seen tears. No, the reason this conversation is so hard to begin is not that it breaks their hearts. It's hard because both the news—and their relative indifference to it—breaks mine.

In attempting to understand their reactions, I've tried to recall how *I* felt as child when I received the news of a death, but my own memories are vague—and I can only assume that they are vague because those deaths made little impression. Death might have seemed like something that mainly affected adults or that didn't touch people near to me. In the years before I became a teenager, people we knew must have died. Surely. But if it upset me at all, the impression was too shallow to stick with me into adulthood.

I do recall trying to drum up tears for my grandfather on the day I heard the news of his passing. Even though he had lived next door to us during his final years, he had never spent individual time with me that I could recall, and we weren't close. Still, I wished I could feel *some* twinge of grief. Other members of my family had tears. My grandmother cried. I did feel unhappy—not so much because of my own grief, but because of the *pressure* to feel grief. I knew enough to understand that tears were an appropriate response, but my eyes were unable to wring out a drop. What I felt was not sorrow so much as discomfort. In fact, I can think of no experience so completely unsettling to my young self as seeing the adults around me cry.

There's an old song called "Hard-Hearted Hannah" about a murderous woman with all the empathy of a granite countertop. Now I'm pretty sure I never killed a man for fun, but my dad used to bring up the title of that song to joke about my lack of emotional tenderness. He was, no doubt, onto something. It's probably true that my ability to enter into other people's emotions—especially to express sorrow—was subpar when compared with my peers. Maybe I truly was stone-hearted. I wonder. Or was I simply a kid?

I do know that, to this day, I find myself glancing around for the nearest fire exit whenever a feverish display of emotion—regardless of what emotion it is—starts to heat up the room. And if I ever sense that someone is trying to draw on my feelings—whether of guilt or grief or motherly love—to elicit a particular response from me (to make a donation or buy life insurance) my defenses drop into place like an iron portcullis. *You shall not pass.*

For good or ill, there are few kinds of interaction that I despise more than emotional manipulation, even when it's well meant. And big, public displays of emotion downright scare me.

At certain worship services I've attended, there's often a moment in the praise chorus that literally makes me shudder. Physically. I dread it. It's that moment when the worship band suddenly pauses for two heartbeats, right before the key change. I shudder because I know that this is the moment when all the dear people around me will spontaneously—at the same time—lift their hands and close their eyes with upturned faces and start to sway with the passionate tide. When I can see that emotional swell forming and rolling toward me, it makes me want to run for dry ground or hide under the theater seating before the wave breaks and tries to pull me under. It's hard not to panic. Even after it's over, I feel a bit resentful, like I've been pummeled by the wave of emotion and then left to stand by myself, dripping and covered in sea grime. Rock concerts and inspirational speakers and feel-good movie endings make me uncomfortable for the same reason; I can see what's coming, and all I want is to pile up dry, rational sandbags as a levy against the rising emotional flood.

My mistrust of emotional excess has its benefits. It's proven invaluable in resisting peer pressure, manipulation, and the kind of unhealthy sentimentalism that doesn't want babies to ever grow up or that dreams impossible dreams that can only disappoint. But my dread of emotional displays is sometimes misplaced. God created us to be emotional beings. Emotional experiences are one of the powerful means by which we connect to other people and even to our God—who describes Himself and His dealings with us in emotional terms—anger, jealousy, grief, pity, joy, delight, and so on—in various places in Scripture. So, I have to remind myself that emotion itself is not the problem, but emotion divorced from wisdom and self control.

I do sometimes wonder if what I often think of as my "emotional maturity" is nothing more than fear of vulnerability—emotional self-protection at the expense of deeper relationships. I want to cultivate true maturity, not fear and constant distrust, in myself and my kids. And I don't always know myself well enough to discern whether I'm wisely resisting manipulation or stubbornly resisting emotional connection with others. What I hope I am learning to do is to concede that emotional experience can be a powerful good. I want my emotions, when appropriate, to be a river that runs clear and deep. What I do not want is for my emotions to slosh over their banks, get muddied with a little sin and a little folly, pull me under, and wash me out to sea.

At funerals, in particular, I have begun to realize that I might truly need those moments when my feelings are drawn out in ways I'm tempted to resist. Those photo slide shows that are so common at twenty-first century funerals are, in a way, calculated to make people cry. But I surprise myself by realizing that this kind of "manipulation" can do a great deal of cathartic good. Could it be that these PowerPoint displays and the sappy music that so often accompanies them are doing for us what professional mourners used to do in Jesus' day—creating an emotional atmosphere that allows people who truly need to grieve to do so openly and without shame?

Even so—with music and slideshows and bad news and all—my children rarely cry over loss of life. I sometimes wish they would. I try to set the appropriate mood. I suppose you could say that I try to manipulate them, through my facial expressions and tone of voice, into feeling a particular way. But from what I remember about myself, and from what I've observed in kids generally, the ability to

truly grieve grows out of life experiences that most kids—
at least most kids in this time and place—simply haven't
lived through. And that may not be such a bad thing.

ONE SUNDAY AT OUR CHURCH IN DALLAS, AN
elderly retired pastor-substitute taught our adult Sunday
school class while our regular pastor was on vacation.
Pastor Thorpe prefaced his lesson by warning us that he
might tear up, and he begged our pardon in advance. He
told us that he didn't preach or teach much anymore because the more he aged, the more he was given to tears.
The sentence was hardly out of his mouth before his eyes
welled up, and he had to pull out a tissue. "That's what
happens when you get old," he said with an awkward
laugh after blowing his nose. The older you get, he told
us, the more you find that everything—the sad things and
the beautiful things—can make you cry.

I fear that he's right.

I'm still a mostly dry-eyed gal, but the ocular flood-
gates aren't holding back the water quite as reliably as
they used to. Until I had children, I was, as you know,
almost completely indifferent to babies. Not anymore. I
now find tears trying to leak through at the mere sight
of a newborn infant. I cannot explain why in fully rational terms, but I think that, with the added years, I have
known too much of childbearing and child-rearing to be

indifferent. I have experienced what it means to bring a child into this world—with all the pain and joy, all the struggle and triumph, that it represents. The lump in my throat testifies that with each first breath, the world will never be the same.

I now choke up during baptisms. Graduations give me goosebumps. Weddings are even worse. So much Kleenex. But at funerals? There, I've discovered, in just the last few years since Jonah's diagnosis, that every vestige that remains of my stoic Scandinavian heritage tries to abandon me.

During the most recent graveside service I attended, I could not seem to keep hold of even the smallest thread of emotional equanimity. We were supposed to sing, but my voice kept cracking, so I had to quit and just mouth what words I could. By the time we had lined up to greet the family, I couldn't speak at all on account of the sob I was desperately choking back. I fought the tears, but they fought harder. I honestly don't know why I bother to fight them anymore. What's the purpose? Water conservation? To save the mascara?

Yes. I'm sure it's for the mascara.

I DO BELIEVE THAT EMOTIONAL SELF-CONTROL is evidence of growing maturity. The older they get, the more I do expect my kids to resist the urge to collapse on the floor and howl over the color of plastic cup they've been given at breakfast. Similarly, I expect them to learn—over time—that it is good, right, and beneficial to contain their giddy excitement. Not all emotional mayhem comes in the form of a tantrum; happiness can bring folly of a different sort. My kids are more than welcome to experience happy feelings over the good things in life, but they need not express them by sprinting around the living room, jumping on the furniture, and giggling like deranged hyenas.

Maturity does mean learning to bridle the emotions and rein them in. Proverbs says that it's the fool who vents all his feelings and the wise man who holds them back (29:11). But, at the same time, expressions of joy and sorrow are not merely human; they are divine. Our Savior wept at the death of His friend. He wept over the city of Jerusalem. Our God rejoices over us with singing. He sits in the heavens and laughs. There really *is* a time to cry and a time to laugh, a time to grieve and a time to dance (John 11:35, Luke 19:41, Zeph. 3:17, Ps. 2:4, Eccles. 3:4).

Fools express their joy and grief without restraint, without wisdom, without maturity. This is something I've understood for as long as I can remember. There really is a kind of emotional expression that must be resisted.

But I've realized as I've gotten older that time and wisdom bring with them the somewhat paradoxical gift of empathy. For me to rejoice with those who rejoice and to weep with those who weep has required a maturing imagination—the ability to enter into the experience of what the other is feeling and to feel it *with* them.

I REMEMBER AFTERNOONS SPENT PLAYING "orphans" as a little girl with my friend from school. In the safety and security of home, it was a thrill to be on our own, fending for ourselves, pretending to hunt for nuts and berries in imaginary winter woods. *Orphan*, to us, meant freedom and adventure, and there would be chocolate chip cookies from Mom when we were done. But to children in different circumstances, the word *orphan* would mean something else entirely—something too bleak for any game.

Only as an adult and as a mother has the plight of true orphans taken on emotional shape. Every time my husband and I leave for a weekend trip without our children and pray for safety on the road, I can feel the devastation wrapped up within that word *orphan*. It defies the rules of phonics and sounds instead like squealing tires and breaking glass and collapsing steel. I am grateful that my children's ears remain deaf to it.

For some children, grief descends early and often—a burden too heavy for their small arms to carry—making every subsequent sorrow into an additional weight dropped upon an already cracked and fragile frame. However, my upbringing in a safe, loving, unthreatened and unthreatening home made it nearly impossible to feel deep sorrow for anyone else because I could not begin to imagine what the sorrowing person was feeling; I had never felt it for myself. Divorce, abuse, abandonment, and death might as well have existed on another planet. And the way the children of those experiences sometimes behaved made them seem almost as alien. Their strange means of expression, their clinginess or inwardness or wild outbursts were all a kind of foreign language that I did not wish to learn.

There are depths of grief, as well as depths of joy, to which no child I know can safely swim; he will return to the surface, if he does not drown, with a case of the emotional bends.

It took becoming a wife for me to imagine the grief of someone who has lost a spouse. It took becoming a mother for me to recognize the extent of the heartbreak a parent could feel at the loss of a child. I had to walk with friends through the life-shattering experience of losing a loved one before I could fully appreciate the extent to which death can upend the lives of those left behind. It took having a child with cancer to understand the shock and dismay a parent can feel at receiving hard news about her child. It has taken time and experience to learn how to enter into the joy and the grief of those around me, and I am only just beginning to understand how best to love others through it.

THE FIRST TIME I REMEMBER FIGHTING BACK actual tears in the face of death was when a classmate—one I hardly knew, although his mother was one of my junior high PE teachers—died of leukemia.

I remember sitting in a circle on the gym floor and being told that Dirk Peterson was in Seattle at the hospital being treated for leukemia after a blood test had revealed something scary. I knew nothing about leukemia, but I did know that it involved many, many needles. And I certainly knew what a fear of needles was like. Just the thought of a blood test gave me the heebie-jeebies. I honestly don't think I could have imagined anything more horrifying than coming down with an illness that involved facing multiple needles. Empathy is exactly what I felt that day.

Our seventh-grade class skipped PE that afternoon to sit on the gym floor and scrawl our greetings with bright Crayola markers on giant get-well cards made from sheets of poster board. As weeks passed, our teachers would give us periodic reports on Dirk's health. The school year progressed and ended, and I forgot all about Dirk for a time. My family moved overseas for a year, and I lost track of his story.

Back in the states, at the start of my ninth-grade year, I learned that Dirk had died during the summer. I don't remember how I felt at hearing the news. What I do remember was a little ceremony held at the back of the

school by the picnic tables. I remember kids crying in the
hallway afterward, and I remember an announcement
that a grief counselor would be available for us to talk to
and that we would be allowed to skip class to do so. One
older kid joked to a friend that he was going to take any
excuse he could get to skip class, even it meant having to
talk to a grief counselor. (I have little doubt that that kid
has come into his own share of grief since then.)

Not until that little ceremony did Dirk's death finally
strike an emotional chord—or at least pluck an untuned
emotional string. Glancing around at teachers with swol-
len eyes, seeing girls with their heads bowed and arms
around each other, I understood something of the pain
of death that I hadn't fully recognized before. This boy,
whom I'd last seen running through the school gym,
shooting hoops on the asphalt, and laughing in the cafeteria, was gone, and his absence was breaking the hearts
of the people standing near me. I looked at their stricken
faces, and I felt my own eyes begin to burn. The tears,
unwanted as they were, helped to put out that fire.

THE ONE TIME I REMEMBER ANY OF MY CHIL-
dren crying over a death outside our family was when a
man whom they'd met at the nursing home, whom everyone called "Big Ed," died of cancer. He used to give my
boys little treats when they'd visit him. He'd start to cry

just to see them walk into his room, and then he'd cry to see them leave. When—on the day before our own Jonah was diagnosed with cancer—we learned that Big Ed had died of cancer, our seven-year-old, Paul, cried off and on for hours. But to this day, I don't know what was at the root of his tears. Was it the unexpected loss of a dear old man, or was it that Paul no longer knew someone who would give him quarters to buy Sprite from the pop machine? I suspect it may have been a little of both. The latter *sounds* heartless, and coming from an adult, it would be, but in reality, I think it's merely childlike.

One of the ways children first understand that they are loved is through simple physical tokens—food, warmth, and gentle touch, then small gestures and treats that remind them of the sweetness of our relationship. The one thing I inherited from my grandmother after her death is the one thing that, as a child, had meant the most to me of anything she owned: a red, cast iron gumball machine. My grandfather had rigged it so that it no longer required pennies; simply turn the crank to make it give birth to one (or, if you were lucky, two) of its glossy, slightly stale gumballs. It sat on top of Grandma's piano, ready to dispense sweetness to us kids at the end of a long road trip to her house. Upon our arrival, gum and grandmotherly love were virtually indistinguishable.

It was kindness translated into sugar that my not-yet-mature soul could best understand.

All of that to say, when I try to deliver news of the death of a child to my boys, it's hard for me, but I'm not sure what I should expect of them. I've found myself wishing they felt the gravity of the news or had the decency to shed a tear, or—at very least—shake their heads sadly and mope for a bit. But why?

Why would I wish deeper heartache upon them? Their capacity for grief, as well as their capacity for joy, will grow with their years. Why should I try to impose man-sized grief upon child-sized hearts?

Dozens of times I have run through in my mind what it would be like to lose a child, and it is not a scenario that I can play out in my imagination without feeling my lungs deflate and my heart pound and my eyes burn. When I think of these children's mothers going to bed that first night after kissing their child's soft forehead for the last time, I cannot find words adequate to express the pain in a way my children could ever understand. Nor would I want to.

I push away the image from my mind, breathe slowly, and tell my children the simple facts: "Remember X from the children's hospital? Well, I just learned that he died this week."

"Really? Oh man. Too bad . . . Can we have mac and cheese for lunch?"

I can still picture soft-spoken Alicia, with her olive skin, resting her bald head on her mother's shoulder in the waiting room. I often remember sweet, smiley Marleigh with her huge blue eyes, giggling as Paul pulled her through the hospital hallways in a plastic wagon. I sometimes think of the tiny girl whose name I've forgotten, but whose image is still burned into my memory—her hair gone, her face marked by skin lesions, her brow furrowed with focused attention as she struggled to learn to use crutches after her lower leg had been amputated due to an aggressive osteosarcoma. All of these children are gone, along with many others, and I have ached for them and for their families as I broke the news to my boys.

But there is one death that stands out to me because it was both far away and as near as my own heart.

When we began using the *#prayforjonah* hashtag online so that friends could keep track of updates on our son, I discovered that on the other side of the country there was another Jonah, nearly the same age as my Jonah, who was also was battling leukemia. He, too, loved baseball. He, too, attended a Christian school that was actively involved in raising funds for his family. He, too, had friends who had printed up a pile of T-shirts— T-shirts that, just like ours, were gray and printed with same message—"Team Jonah"—in white letters across the front. He, too, was going bald and missing his family and longing to run the bases again.

Following his story was like seeing my Jonah's reflection in one of the funhouse mirrors that sits just outside our oncology clinic office. The story was the same—but altered. The parallels were unsettling, and then—they were no more.

My Jonah lived. The other Jonah died.

The morning that I read the news of his death, the feeling that struck me was more like guilt than anything else. *Why that Jonah and not mine? Why is that Jonah's mother selecting music for a funeral while I listen to my Jonah practicing music for a recital? I've been laughing while she's been grieving.* The pity I felt was deep, and yet I could not weep for her son and rejoice for mine in the same breath. Every time I've used the #prayforjonah tag since then, I think of the other Jonah. And as much as it hurt to think of him at first, what I now feel is gratitude. I'm thankful for my son's life. It gives me joy. And I cannot, or *will* not, stifle that joy out of a false respect for another mother's grief. It is her grief that, in some sense, makes my joy stand out in higher relief—her grief that keeps me from taking my joy for granted.

It's a paradox the way other people's suffering and loss can, in the same breath, make us weep and make us deeply thankful. Grief gives birth to gratitude. This juxtaposition of one person's joy and another person's sorrow is woven all through the experience not only of hospital life, but of all of life. While one child is ringing the "end of treatment" bell and celebrating the end of cancer and the return to life, another child down the hall is taking his end-of-life breath.

This contrast—of one man's joy and another man's pain—is often a source for far too much false guilt, particularly in the age of social media. In any given moment, among our hundreds of Facebook friends, there's bound to be at least one who is struggling with some sort of heartbreak. So, out of sensitivity to them, we're told to be careful sharing—or to even *avoid* sharing—our reasons to celebrate. We're told to tone back the happy engagement photos, because some people are dealing with loneliness and divorce. Birth announcements rub salt in the wounds of the childless and bereaved. So we are urged to never do anything but weep with those who weep, and to weep with those who rejoice. Just weep. All the time. Public rejoicing is tone deaf and insensitive.

Nonsense.

I understand the desire to find the right time and place to say something. But we *should* feel joy. And we should be able to invite others to join us in it. We cannot ignore a friend's suffering, and we may need to share our happy news gently, but we do not better honor the dead or comfort the suffering by refusing to honor the living or to rejoice in God's gifts. Godly joy does not gloat over the grieving, certainly. But godly grief must not guilt-trip the joyful.

Refusing to rejoice with those who rejoice does nothing to improve our ability to weep with those who weep. I believe it does quite the opposite. True rejoicing expands and trains our hearts and imaginations to come alongside the grieving—and vice versa. Before I experienced the joy of motherhood, I simply did not have the imaginative experience that would allow me to weep with a grieving mother. My motherly joy is what finally broadened my soul enough to weep over the loss of that joy. Our sensibilities must mature, not in order to level every grief and every joy to a kind of gray, inoffensive apathy, but to both grieve *and* rejoice deeply, wisely, and to the full.

TWO SUMMERS AGO, MY JONAH—MY LEUKEMIA survivor—put on his cleats and glove, and stepped out onto the field for the opening game of the Dirk Peterson Baseball Tournament, named in honor of that boy who died of leukemia all those years ago when I was in middle school. When the baseball game began, my heart rejoiced to see my son take the mound and wind up to pitch. It brings me *more* joy than it once did in the days before he got sick, precisely because I have seen how his story could have ended.

After the game, I took Jonah over to Dirk's parents and introduced him, telling them his story, and sharing my own scant, middle-school memories of Dirk's life. Once again, I was telling my son the story of another child's death—a child very much like himself. But this was different. Dirk's dad gripped my boy's hand, shook it with firm good will, and gave him a few pointers on the art of pitching. Dirk's mother smiled warmly, laughed with us, and thanked us sincerely for taking the time to meet them and to remember Dirk. In expressing my joy over my boy who lived, I found an opportunity I might never have had to honor the boy who died.

I had hardly known Dirk, and he had died when he and I were younger than Jonah is now, so I did not expect my boy to be moved to tears by their story. Nor did they expect Jonah to be. Even with the passage of the years, I know that the loss of their child must leave a chronic ache. But our joy and their grief are not enemies. They never were.

True joy is never the enemy of godly grief. Joy is what trains and equips us to bear it.

CHAPTER 13

Mid(dle School) - Life Crisis

L ooking back to those years in middle school, I remember my life as a series of minor disturbances
that seemed, at the time, to be major. Regardless of who
you are, those preteen and early teen years are likely to
be fraught with uncertainties and can feel like little more
than a rapid succession of seismic shocks—of both body
and soul.

As a young (and maybe not-so-young) girl, what I
dreaded most was an encounter with anything new—new
foods, new sports, new people, new places, new experiences of all sorts. Nothing frightened me more than the
Great Unknown. So when my parents broke the news
that my father had been awarded both a USAID grant to

work in East Africa and a Fulbright Scholarship for research in post-communist eastern Europe—and that we
would be moving to both places in the same year—you
can probably imagine how well I received it. I think I said
something to the effect of "I'm not going." (I was twelve.)

The year before we moved overseas, my parents had
decided to take me out of my little Christian school and
put me into the much bigger public school on the opposite side of town. It was a startling decision, and I
faced the change with a fair bit of stubborn resistance.
But I would have my best friend, Cordelia, there with
me to ease the transition. Or at least that's the thought
that kept me from completely freaking out about ven-
turing into such unfamiliar territory. However, once I
was enrolled, aside from occasionally passing her in the
halls between classes, I never saw her at school, not even
during lunch.

I made few friends in seventh grade. I had the double disadvantage of being the shy, unfashionable new girl
and of having come from a school that, I was informed,
was full of rich kids and snobs. (If only they knew how
many parents scrimped and saved and took second and
third jobs delivering newspapers and driving buses just
to give their kids a Christian education.) The only people
who really did welcome me into this socially stratified
new world were the "goth" kids—the ones all dressed in
black, with punk T-shirts and home-dyed hair and safety

pins for earrings. I was both shy and lonely. And they? Unlike the cool girls—who spent the lunch hour comparing how many pairs of Guess jeans they owned, and who ignored me after I said "none"—these misfits with their dark capes and heavy eyeliner always had a spot for me at the lunch table and never treated me with disdain. They looked creepy, but they were kind. So I was grateful.

For the most part, however, I kept quietly to myself and managed to survive that awkward school year, but I was by no means excited about returning for eighth grade. Besides, my friend Cordelia's dad had just accepted a job in Ohio, thousands of miles away, which meant that the one true friend I did have there would not be coming back. So I suppose the news that my family would be leaving, too, should have come as a relief, but it didn't.

I worried. I argued. I tried to invent reasons to move in with my grandparents so that I could go on living the same uneventful life, such as it was, that I'd come to know. I didn't love the school situation, but at least it had become familiar. So I prayed that something would arise that would require me to stay right where I was. But the answer to that prayer turned out to be a resounding *no*. God had other plans.

By the time summer rolled around, my mom had purchased a set of cassette tapes and a bilingual dictionary, and we spent a half-hour each day sitting at the table trying to learn how to say hello and ask for directions in

Serbo-Croatian. I must not have applied myself to the effort because I remember nothing. But I do remember spending many hours thumbing slowly through travel guides to Kenya and Yugoslavia, imagining what it must feel like to attend school in the African highlands or to wake up inside an apartment in Sarajevo.

Adults always talked about the importance of cultivating imagination in children. But my highly cultivated imagination was doing a terrific job of composing vivid and lifelike scenes filled with all kinds of desolation and misery. I had carefully painted a picture of my future, and I was not liking what I saw.

By mid-summer, the news coming from the Balkans was exactly the kind of news the world has come to expect from the Balkans: border disputes, civil unrest, protests, outbreaks of violence. The U.S. Embassy in Yugoslavia was on high alert, and my dad's Fulbright research was looking more and more uncertain.

I felt a small wave of relief, thinking that a war in that part of the world could be an answer to my prayers to stay in this part of the world. (Does self-centeredness have no limits?) The problem was, our house was already rented out for the year. A family with three boys had signed a one-year lease, so we were expected to be out before the start of the new school year. My dad finally received word that we should hold off on plans to travel to Yugoslavia until the situation could resolve, but with no place to call home, we drove across Washington and moved in with my mom's parents. My brother and I started homeschooling, and we kept up with our Serbo-Croatian language lessons, right up until a few days before all-out war broke out at our intended destination. Travel plans were canceled, research terms were revised, and the Fulbright program scrambled to find an alternative eastern European location where my dad could proceed with his studies on post-communist freedom of the press.

This waiting process did not help my nervous jitters in the least. Military families who have been bounced all over the world, from one base to the next, with little advance notice, probably know this experience well. But knowing we would be going somewhere foreign—and not knowing where—gave me a sick feeling in my gut. I really just wanted to stay at Grandma's house for the rest of the year.

At last, word came from the Fulbright office that my dad would become the next research scholar to Poland, which meant that our family would soon be packing our bags again and flying to our newly selected home in Warsaw. There, in a two-bedroom apartment without a stove or an oven or a dishwasher or a washing machine, we would be spending the gray and snowy months of October, November, and December. What middle-class American teenager wouldn't be thrilled?

We arrived, bleary-eyed, at the Warsaw airport after a series of long red-eye flights—including a final leg on a German airline, which seated us in the row immediately behind the smoking section and served us a morning meal of rye bread, limp vegetables, and some kind of deli loaf made of jellied fish, plus a personal bottle of wine. (Breakfast of champions.) My fifth-grade brother, Ethan, and I picked at it with mixed horror and laughter—the kind of giggles you get only when you're incredibly tired or uncommonly nervous.

I'm sure Poland is a lovely country in the green and flowered months of June and July, but I have never witnessed it, so I'll just have to take other people's word. What I saw when we stepped out of the terminal and onto the sidewalk outside the airport was gray. Gray in every conceivable direction. The sky was gray. The earth was gray. The snow was a dirty gray. The buildings were gray. And nearly every individual on the street wore some shade of khaki, black, or gray.

While the months we spent in Poland were, of course, not all bad, *gray* is the feeling that permeates many of the memories from that cold, dreary season.

Our first night in Warsaw, before our apartment was ready, was spent at the MDM Hotel near the center of the city. Despite the snow swirling in eddies outside the lobby door, the building, we were told, would not be heated until after three consecutive days of freezing temperatures—a regulation left over from the all-too-recent days when this had been a government-run communist outfit. The whole establishment, in fact, was a bad hangover from a half-century spent drinking deep of communist bureaucracy. Every space in the hotel smelled of cheap cigarettes, and the rooms were cold enough that we could see our breath. Our mattresses lay on bed frames that had been built at an incline on one end—to ensure a "healthy" angle that would aid with "proper breathing." Our room had a view of a large town square over which hung a huge neon sign advertising "Wełna" (wool) and a billboard for Bulgarian wine. In a nearby window, a red and white flag emblazoned with *Solidarność* filled the glass.

The sun rose at ten and set at four. During our stay in Poland, there were days when the sun itself seemed to have had the life sucked from it, days when color film was a superfluous commodity. Countless pitiable souls stumbling along the side streets had given themselves over to fifths of cheap vodka in their pursuit of a remedy to the chill without and the darkness within. We felt the oppression of that winter ourselves.

It was no small feat adjusting to these new surroundings. My mother washed laundry in a bathtub filled with the red-brown tap water that issued from our aging pipes. And once, while getting up from her knees, she slipped and fractured her rib against the edge of the tub and spent much of our Christmas vacation wincing in pain. (It did help that we escaped to Marseilles, France, on the sunny Mediterranean, for the holiday.) And to dry our clothes, she hung them outside on our apartment balcony, only to bring them indoors frozen stiff. We propped pairs of iced blue jeans against the wall like a row of boards.

An avid baker, she resorted to steaming bread inside a soup pot on our hot plate. Shopping was a tangled business fraught with language hurdles and unfamiliar foodstuffs that had to be hauled home on foot with a cardboard box strapped to a luggage cart across several sets of railroad tracks and down a pitted gravel road spotted with mud and snow. Once, the wheel of our cart caught as we crossed the tracks, and the whole thing tipped, landing a poorly wrapped package of meat into the mud and transforming a bottle of Pepsi—meant as a surprise treat—into a fizzing puddle filled with shards of broken glass. As my mom and I stooped next to the rail line to recover what was salvageable from our groceries, irritated Poles sidestepped us and hurried past on their way to catch the tram. It was the only time in my whole childhood that I can remember ever seeing my mother walk in the door to our home and collapse on the couch in tears.

Sure, it could have been worse. Much worse. But still, this was not exactly the sophisticated "semester abroad" or the romantic "European experience"—or even the charmingly Instagrammable "mission trip"—that most people sign up for, either. I felt displaced and lonely and terribly homesick. I think all of us did, to varying degrees.

Looking back, I can at least say that none of us wishes we hadn't gone. My dad was able to do some very valuable research and meet scores of interesting people at the university. We visited beautiful palaces and churches and museums. We met remarkable people, including one silver-haired man, a Jew, who had survived a death march across Europe in the winter—after serving in the Polish resistance, being forced at gunpoint to live in the Jewish ghetto, and being imprisoned in a German concentration camp during the second World War. Parts of history I had only heard about were taking concrete shape in this place. And we did find plenty of fun and funny ways to pass the time, whether exploring the city or playing games at home. God was certainly with us through hours of both homesickness and happiness.

Some of our happiest moments were spent among the church family we had joined. We found a tiny English-speaking Methodist congregation that was attended by dear people from all over the world. To meet fellow English speakers in Poland was always a delightful surprise. But to find fellow English speakers who were also fellow believers was like finding water in the desert. In a place where nearly all of us felt somewhat homeless, this small weekly gathering of protestant Christians was like coming home to family, and our various Baptist and

Methodist and Presbyterian differences faded into insignificance. That church service was the highlight of my week. We worshipped together and often stayed to eat lunch together at a "milk bar" nearby. There were no kids my age or my brother's age among them. In fact, there seemed to be no kids our ages in the entire city of Warsaw. But I truly didn't care, so long as we had people to talk to in our own tongue, people with whom we could worship the same God. Members of that tiny congregation have remained in contact with my parents to this day.

Finding this church was one of the many delightful ways in which we saw God's care for us amid some less-than-idyllic months. But the happiest surprise—the one that stands out most from our life in Poland and the one that we have retold more than any other—was on a weekend trip outside Warsaw.

My parents had decided that before we left the country, we should visit Kraków, which has long been considered the best-preserved and loveliest city in Poland. So one weekend in late November or early December, we boarded the train from Warsaw and set out to explore this historic city. When we arrived, we visited the "cloth hall" (the old covered market at the center of the city), stopped to see Saint Mary's Basilica, passed through the old city gates, climbed Wawel Hill to retrace the centuries-old footsteps of the kings and nobles of Poland, and looked out across the old city and the river below. But on the second and last night of our visit, the weather had taken a nasty turn. Rain fell and froze on every surface it touched, turning the old town square, now almost entirely cleared of people, into a broad, cobbled ice rink. We stood, huddled under a street lamp, flipping hurriedly through a Kraków guidebook in search of a place to warm up and eat our dinner before returning to our hotel.

While we stood there, my dad looked up and noticed a man standing, like us, under a street lamp on the far side of the square and holding a map at an old-man distance from his eyes.

"Look over there," he told us. We looked. "Does that guy look familiar?"

My dad cleaned his rain-spattered glasses and looked again. "Huh. He kinda does," he said. So we cautiously shuffled across the ice in his direction, trying to look casual, in case we were mistaken and were headed toward a complete stranger. But as we slid closer, the man's profile became clearer, and we knew for certain who was standing there in the lamplight: Amos Yoder. He was a professor emeritus from the same university where my dad taught back in Idaho. He was also a member of our church back home. We didn't know him well, but the sight of him in this strange land and stranger circumstance seemed almost miraculous. "Amos?" my dad said when we were near enough to be heard.

He looked toward us and started to laugh. "Roy?"

Before we had left home, my dad had heard that Dr. Yoder was traveling overseas, but didn't know details. It turned out that he was now living in Hungary, also on a Fulbright scholarship, and he had crossed the border to visit Kraków for just the one afternoon and was headed back that night. We were there for just two days. And now, half a world away from our little Idaho town, in an abandoned city square, in the midst of an ice storm, in the dark, at dinnertime, our paths had crossed. Of all places to find a familiar face, this would surely seem to be the last. But here we stood.

We found a restaurant there in the old town that had once been a favorite dining spot for fourteenth-century royalty. It was a dimly lit building with arched doors and ceilings and walls hung with gilt-framed paintings as wide as a bus, and we ate together, swapping stories of Hungary and Warsaw and home. Then Dr. Yoder followed us to our humble little hotel room, where he dried his wet socks on our radiator and then left to catch the train back to Budapest. The following morning, we returned to our Warsaw flat. And I returned convinced that, while we had made our plans, God had, for some reason, guided our steps (Prov. 16:9) toward that one place in that one moment to give us that one strange, brief taste of home.

I'd be lying to say that that single experience gave me a sunny disposition toward the remainder of our days in Poland. But after that surprise meeting, I did see more clearly that God was with us in a way I hadn't recognized before—guiding us, even through ice and storm and dark of night, according to His perfect plans.

CHAPTER 14

Don't Drink the Water

After our three months in Warsaw, we headed south to Kenya, where we planned to spend the rest of the academic year. Leaving Poland, I was more nervous than I had been when we prepared to leave the United States. My main concern this time was school. In Poland, as I mentioned, we very rarely ran into kids of any age. I don't know why that was, but the sight of another child, whether in the market or on the bus or anywhere else, was a rare occurrence. And the few encounters we did have with other kids made me incredibly uncomfortable on account of the language barrier. Truth be told, encounters with other kids usually made me nervous even without the language barrier.

I had always tended to prefer the company of adults to spending time with peers. Adults seemed more predictable, more logical, more sane. Just to avoid the loud and erratic behavior of the other kids at one of my own childhood birthday parties, I hid in my parents' closet during a game of hide-and-seek and did not come out until the other guests started to leave. In retrospect, it's a wonder I had friends at all. Given my tendency to avoid unnecessary contact with groups of unfamiliar children, homeschooling during those few months in Warsaw had been a comfort; it allowed me to avoid having to meet new people away from the buffer formed by my outgoing brother and my parents. But in Kenya, Ethan and I would once again be in separate classrooms and attending, as day students, a British boarding school where I didn't know a soul—and where I wouldn't have a single social crutch to lean on.

In addition to my social anxiety, I also had a hard time shaking the mental image that had been so adroitly painted by all of those sponsor-a-child charity organizations back in the states. When I thought of Africa, I thought of dusty landscapes punctuated with mud huts and skinny cattle, where starving orphans ate watery mush out of plastic bowls while flies hovered around their sad eyes. Those photos exist because that poverty really does exist in parts of Africa. And it *is* sad. But my dad was going there to teach at a university, for pity's sake. And starving, famine-stricken societies do not build institutions of higher education. I'd even seen photos of the nearby city, with its paved streets and its sidewalks lined with picturesque blooming jacaranda trees. But without those pictures in front of me, my mind reverted to images of poverty and destitution. I dreaded the day we stepped onto the plane to Kenya.

When we stepped *off* the airplane in Nairobi, however, it was like that scene in *The Wizard of Oz* when Dorothy opens the door of her gray and colorless Kansas home and finds herself in a dazzling and unfamiliar world of brilliant Technicolor. We walked out of the Jomo Kenyatta Airport and entered a world of blue skies, warm sun, and brilliant clusters of magenta and orange bougainvillea spilling over the walls. My mother later described that drive away from the airport as the lifting of a heavy cloud. She hadn't realized how oppressive the sunless Polish skies had been until we touched down in the equatorial sunshine. I didn't feel quite the same sense of relief that she did, but I couldn't deny that the comparison between the two climates did not lean in favor of the Warsaw winter.

The drive through the Kenyan countryside to the town of Njoro was beautiful. The flat-topped acacia trees were unlike anything I'd seen before, and even the humble starlings that landed in the branches glistened with iridescent blues and greens in the uninterrupted sunlight.

But not everything was flowers and sunshine. Upon arriving at our new home, we learned that the university was still in the process of making repairs after a student riot had shut down classes, destroyed property, and left debris scattered around campus. The cause of the riot, we were told, was that the cafeteria was not serving enough chicken.

We—well-fed Americans that we were—laughed at the absurdity of the story, but we later discovered that the incident was symptomatic of deeper troubles stirring beneath the surface. Although we spent only five short months in East Africa, our time there involved a number of unsettling events that left deeper impressions than almost any other period of my life. Some of that was due to my age. Thirteen is already an age of big transitions, but for me that year was also filled with unexpected delights and dangers that were something beyond the ordinary experience of an average girl from Idaho.

SCHOOL TURNED OUT TO BE FAR MORE PLEASant than my brooding teenage apprehensions had pictured. The campus was green and lovely, the teachers were helpful, and the students were friendly almost to a fault. It was an international school, so many of us kids, and most of the teachers as well, were outsiders to some extent, which meant there was a kind of instant camaraderie that came from the shared identity of "foreigner." Even the Kenyans in my class were mostly from other parts of the country. I was the only American—and the only white person—in my class, but I felt more at home there than I had ever felt at the mostly white, all-American public school that I'd left behind in the States. After just a few weeks in our new home, the one thing that I had been most worried about ended up, as is often the case in my life, among my fondest memories. There was still plenty I didn't understand about student life, and I had more than enough catching up to do in subjects that were new to me, but school was, on the whole, a happy experience.

Outside of school, our family also discovered that we had a lot of cultural adjustments to make. In Poland, we had stood out in a crowd on account of our brightly colored clothes in that sea of unbroken gray. We adapted by buying khaki and drab to blend in. But here, we stood out on account of our *lack* of color. And no amount of shopping could change that. When we walked through campus one day, a class of kindergartners met us coming the other way and instantly started pointing and shouting, "*Wazungu! Wazungu!*" ("White people! White people!"). And in the market, vendors would sell a kilo of fruit to the person in front of us for one price, and then to us at a higher price—"*wazungu* price"—without even trying to disguise what they were doing.

We learned that white people tended to be at greater risk for bribery, theft, and attacks by roadside bandits, in part because white people were assumed—often rightly—to have money. Friends told us to avoid driving at night whenever possible. Poorly lit and poorly maintained roads could lead to being stranded. And being stranded would leave anyone, of any skin color, vulnerable to attackers both human and animal.

It was not that we lived our lives there in a state of constant distrust. We shopped, we ate, we went to church, we attended work and school, and we went about the business of daily life just like everyone else we knew. But when we went out in public, we were generally on the alert for possible signs of trouble, and there were, in fact, a number of situations when we were—or believed we were—in real danger.

Most "dangers" were minor. In the city where we shopped, we were often approached by ragged boys with a reputation for picking pockets in order to buy glue to sniff as a cheap drug for a perilous high.

Driving was an act of faith when roads were so broken up with pot holes that many drivers simply turned off the road and drove instead through the dirt and scrub grass along the side for a smoother ride. Sometimes the traffic lights worked. Sometimes they didn't. And even if they did, there was no telling whether the other drivers would actually abide by those signals.

Malaria, carried by mosquitoes, and sleeping sickness, transmitted by biting tsetse flies, were a fairly common concern for which we prepared with daily doses of intensely bitter quinine as well as bed netting and even, sometimes, long sleeves. And water-borne illness could pose an even greater threat. We were careful not to drink or even wash our vegetables in the tap water without boiling and filtering it first. These were fairly minor inconveniences, but once we learned how to take the necessary precautions and to adapt to the new way of life, they ceased to occupy our minds. We had other, more pressing concerns to deal with.

Once, on a trip to Mount Kenya during a school holiday, we and another American family were driving toward the summit through deep, red dust so fine that it billowed into the back seat of our little Datsun Bluebird through the holes where speakers had once been. The cloud of fine grit nearly choked my brother and me and forced us to cover our faces with T-shirts and pillowcases. My dad swerved back and forth to avoid the boulders that rose through the dust in the road, but as we came up over a small rise, he suddenly said, "Uh oh!" He'd seen the boulder in our path too late, and we were going to hit it. We braced for the impact, but nothing happened. "What . . . " Dad began as he looked in the rearview mirror. My mom, brother, and I swiveled in our seats to look behind us. Our tire track ran right through the squashed center of the "boulder." Dad started to laugh. Elephant dung! Those rocks were nothing but fresh elephant dung. "Let's just hope we don't run into the animals who made those!" Dad said, still chuckling. If he was nervous, he didn't show it.

Weeks in advance, my parents had made a reservation to stay somewhere near the top of the mountain, but halfway up the winding dusty road to the summit, in the middle of a bamboo forest so dense it lined the road like a living wall, our car died. Dad tried the ignition several times, but the car simply would not start.

With keys still dangling from the steering column, he pulled the parking brake up with a jerk, stepped out into the red dust, linked his hands behind his neck and exhaled a long, tense breath through puffed cheeks. "What happened?" I asked, hearing the tension in my own voice. "Why won't it start?" Dad was at a loss and struggling to keep his concern and frustration from bubbling to the surface. We were stuck and seemed to have no means of getting unstuck. We all got out and stared blankly at the car, wondering what to do next. The friends we'd been traveling with pulled up alongside us in their safari-tested SUV when they saw the Datsun at a standstill.

They had no extra seats for our family, but Mr. Pals told us he'd drive on ahead and find help if he could, although he wasn't sure how many miles still lay ahead. Could be hours. Could be after dark when he returned.

Could be a bunch of white tourists stranded after nightfall in the middle of a dark forest filled with elephants—and who knows how many armed bandits. But what options did we have?

Mr. Pals hit the gas and drove away around the next bend—where his invincible Isuzu Trooper also sputtered to a stop.

Clearly, walking the rest of the way was not even an option. We weren't even sure if it was safe to get out of our vehicles for more than a few moments. We had no cell phone. Little water. Less food. And we were utterly coated with a layer of sweaty red grime. The only option was to attempt to turn back.

The men took turns behind the wheels of the two cars, slowly turning them to face downhill. Pointed in the right direction, we coasted in neutral down the mountain, through dung piles and dust, trying, at intervals, to wake the engines, until somewhere, several hundred feet from where we had stalled, both cars finally roared back to life.

Lack of oxygen for proper ignition was what they concluded had caused the problem. But now, without a reservation or even a phone with which to make one, we raced against time to find a place to stay the night. After a frantic consultation with maps and guidebooks, we rattled up a rutted dirt driveway to a motel set off from the road and seemingly abandoned. Its empty swimming pool and crumbling gates looked like a scene from a low-budget horror flick, but we breathed relief to see an attendant appear and show us to a couple of cabanas with—hallelujah—actual showers. They were tiny and ran ice cold after the first few moments, but water—unsafe to drink and all—never felt so welcome and fresh as when it washed the sweat-salted dust from our exhausted bodies and accumulated into a layer of red clay half an inch thick around our feet. And I am quite sure I have never felt so grateful to be leaving a "vacation" behind.

ANOTHER TIME, MY BROTHER AND I WERE BE-ing driven home by Makuno, the driver hired by the university to take us to and from school each day. As we drove out of the school grounds and onto the road toward the city of Nakuru that lay between our school and our apartment at the University, we found that we were the only car going that direction. Streaming out of the city, in buses, in donkey carts, on bicycles, and piled into the back of pickups, were hundreds and hundreds of people. They appeared to be fleeing the apocalypse with nothing but the clothes on their hot backs. Our driver pulled off the road to wait and see if the stream of people would slow. It didn't. So he drove a little further and stopped again to ask what was going on.

"Shootings!" someone said.

"Police are shooting guns and using tear gas on the crowd," somebody else added breathlessly.

Makuno sighed and sat quietly for a moment, considering. We had to get through the city somehow to return home, but he wasn't going to risk taking us through a violent riot. So he turned the car around and took us back to wait at the school. I would have called home to let my parents know we would be late, but we had no phone at home. The university had promised us one for months, but all they had delivered was the physical object; it connected to nothing. My dad did have a phone in his office, but none of us knew the number, and I'm not sure it would have mattered. Whenever he tried to mention on the phone that there was civil unrest or other matters of concern about our situation, his line would go dead. So we had no means of contacting my parents, and they had no means of contacting us.

Half an hour later, Makuno corralled us back into the car, and the highway scene we returned to was unchanged—people streaming out of the city by any means possible. We drove back to school once more, waited another hour, and tried again. Same story. The entire city seemed like it must be empty of inhabitants by now, and yet still the river of humanity had not dried up. The sky was starting to get dark, but Makuno decided to try one last option. He leaned over to the glove box, pulled out a map and, with his finger, traced an alternative route completely around the city, through the bush, to the other side of town. The drive took almost an hour, but he brought us safely home just as the lights buzzed to life in the parking lot outside our flat.

When we opened the front door, my parents nearly collapsed with relief. They'd heard the news coming from the city of Nakuru and had heard of people fleeing toward our side of town, as well.

That turned out to be the second-to-last last day we attended school. We returned one last time to say goodbye and pack up our belongings. I cried.

THIS WAS AN ELECTION YEAR, AND TENSIONS were dangerously high among the people of Kenya, especially in some of the outlying areas where tribal animosity was often intense.

One morning, as we were eating breakfast, my dad plopped a newspaper onto the table in front of us. The headline read, "Dogs Eating Rotting Bodies at Molo." Molo was a town about twenty miles away, where a group of young Kalenjin militants were reported to have murdered thousands of Kikuyu tribesmen, and many of the bodies were left unburied, some with arrows still protruding from their flesh. Thousands of others fled in terror from the bloodshed. Some of the grieving family members were neighbors, students, and professors there at our university. One of my father's colleagues had lost a brother or a father or maybe both—I can't now remember—in the massacre.

That was when my dad began in earnest to try to find a way for our family to leave the country ahead of schedule. But nearly every time he'd call the embassy in Nairobi (the one that was bombed six years later—in 1998—by Islamist terrorists, killing more than two hundred people) for help or information, the phone would click off and leave him with a dial tone.

During that same time, our family was reading, of all things, the book of Exodus each night before bed. And through those weeks, strange things happened. My father broke out in boils—horrible, painful sores on his head. And days later, we bought a pineapple from a child who was selling them door to door through our apartment complex. The next morning we walked into a kitchen that was swarming with gnats from floor to ceiling. And each time it began to look as though we would be able to evacuate the country, my parents ran into yet another bureaucratic hurdle. Just to leave Kenya ahead of the date marked on our visas, he had to track down a dozen signatures, including a signature from the president of the country. "I feel like Moses," Dad said, "going back to Pharaoh over and over, demanding that he let my people go! Only instead of the plagues falling on the Egyptians, they're falling on us." And at each step of the process, including simply picking up our mail from the post office, there were self-important officials behind desks demanding a little "chai money" for their services.

At last, after weeks of paperwork and interrupted phone conversations, we were given leave to go.

With our house in Idaho still rented to another family, we had no home to return to, so we would spend the next month of waiting in western Europe and divide our stay among Austria, Norway, and the Netherlands. For that, we needed money. As one last part of our exit, my parents had to convert our Kenyan shillings back to American dollars, but we were again told that we would likely be ripped off if we attempted a direct exchange. So after a little research, my dad decided to invest in some gems that he could re-sell in the States. That final walk through crime-riddled downtown Nairobi, with thousands of dollars in cash on his notably white person, got his heart pumping like few cardio workouts had ever done.

I could describe other events—a night spent sleeping at a Sikh temple on a stretch of empty highway between Nakuru and Mombasa; wandering among twelfth-century Arab ruins in the jungle near the coast, where the blue wings of thousands of butterflies littered the ground like fall leaves; swimming in waters that we later learned were home to deadly sea snakes; sharing friendly meals in people's homes; taking Kiswahili lessons on campus; having our picnic site overrun by chattering monkeys during lunch; watching zebras run alongside our vehicle near a flamingo-filled soda lake; and lions and hippos and warthogs—oh my! But in all of that time, the one thing I don't remember feeling was fear. The fear had all been in the anticipation.

NOT MANY WEEKS BEFORE WE FLEW OUT OF Kenya, news reports trickled in from the United States about riots in Los Angeles. Four white officers had been acquitted for the beating of an unarmed black man, Rodney King, and the angry public backlash left dozens dead, many more wounded, homes and business ransacked, and millions of dollars of property damaged. On hearing the reports, our Kenyan friends simply couldn't understand why we would leave the relative peace and safety of their beautiful nation to return to a country where that kind of death and destruction was going down. If anything, our nation was surely no more peaceful and secure than theirs. Weren't we afraid to go home?

How strange to look at our own reflection for the first time, however smudged or distorted the mirror. Is this what others see when they look at us? And if so, what kind of warped funhouse glass might we be peering through as we try to understand the rest of the world?

A year before, during the first war in Iraq, I had seen an interview with an Iraqi woman who was preparing to return home after her studies in the United States. She talked about the inner-city violence in American and how it scared her. But the interviewer was incredulous. *Her* country was at war! Surely there was no comparison! This Iraqi woman could not make the American reporter understand that hers was a beautiful country and that violence was not the defining characteristic of her home. And besides, the worst of the fighting wasn't even near her town. She talked about gardens and museums and festivals. Could it be that people in the Middle East might sometimes hear sounds that consisted of anything other than the pop of gunfire and the rumble of tanks? Not as far as the TV news was concerned. But she was not afraid to go home.

Of course, we weren't afraid to go home, either. Urban L.A. and rural Idaho were practically different planets. In one place, guns meant rioting and violence; in the other, guns meant recreation and venison. It was here in Kenya, not at home, that we sensed danger. But in spite of the apparent dangers, I do not remember once worrying about my safety. I do not remember being truly afraid. For that, I can only thank God and honor my parents.

It's true that we never came face to face with the violence that was occurring so near our home. We certainly never found ourselves under direct attack. Unlike friends we've made in the years since, we were never forced to flee in the dead of night through dense African jungles where the bite of a viper—or of a guerrilla machine gun—might take a man's life. But the dangers we saw did seem near enough that staying would be unwise. After all, before we moved overseas, we had watched from afar as violent skirmishes in the Balkans had canceled our plans and descended into all-out war. My parents—and the U.S. Embassy in Kenya—did not think it advisable for us to wait and see whether the same chain of events would unfold here. Given the riots, the massacres, and the unrest brewing, the prudent thing to do was to leave the country. However, I don't remember ever hearing my mother or father panic in front of my brother and me. I never saw them wringing their hands.

We prayed a lot, sure. Fervently. But never did they fill our home with a spirit of fear. They trusted in God's care.

In seeing God's mercy toward us through all that we'd already experienced, and in seeing my parents' unwavering faith in God's goodness, I was learning to trust Him, too. Technically, we had become evacuees, but when we boarded the plane I honestly felt more regret than relief. I already missed my school and the friends I had made there during our brief stay. I would miss the ibises in the trees and the flamingos in the lake, the acacias and bougainvilleas and jacarandas growing along the road, and even the monkeys terrorizing our picnic table. As the great wide Rift Valley disappeared below the clouds, I truly wished we could have stayed longer. But now we were off to new adventures, and my young heart was—remarkably—at peace.

CHAPTER 15

Stranger in a Strange Kitchen

During the months that my family lived in Kenya, the international boarding school I attended was filled with students not only of many nationalities and ethnicities, but also of many different faiths.

I was the only non-boarder, the only American, the only white student, and one of only a few Protestant Christians in my class. Having arrived halfway through my eighth-grade year, I was also the only kid trying to play catch-up in multiple subjects. I was two years behind in French and German classes, struggling to figure out chemistry abbreviations, attempting to learn swimming strokes and field hockey rules, and scrambling to speed-read the chapters I'd missed in *The Lord of the Flies*.

After a couple of months, I was beginning to understand some of the manners and customs that shaped life at the school, but no hour of the day presented a steeper learning curve than lunchtime. Through a series of social blunders and stern instructions, I had learned to wait to sit until our teacher sat, to eat with my fork always in my left hand and my knife in my right, and never to call pudding *dessert* as I would at home. I had also learned that here, food choices were determined by more than a simple matter of preference. Food, in fact, could be a source of outright terror.

When the lunch bell rang, the girls from my form two class would collect in the white-walled dining hall where equatorial sunlight usually lay in bright streaks across the heavy wooden tables and the polished concrete floor. The double doors on either side of the room were left open to the breeze—a long breath of eucalyptus and red earth and grass still damp from the drenching Kenyan rains.

Our French teacher presided over our table. She stood alone at our head, beautiful with her sun-freckled cheeks and long brown curls, hardly looking older than us thirteen- and fourteen-year-old girls. She would bow her head slightly for the usual hastily mumbled, "Bless us, and these thy gifts, which we receive from thy bountiful goodness"—a brief prayer that seemed calculated to be generic enough to offend few and to please none.

After a half-hearted chorus of *amens*, she sat carefully and stiffly. We sat loudly and awkwardly, all squeaking chair legs and gesticulating arms and angular teenage knees beneath our green uniform skirts.

We poured glasses of iced lemon squash from a plastic pitcher, and our conversations trickled lazily around the table, changing accents as they flowed from girl to girl while we waited for the food to arrive. Some days—perhaps drawn by the hope of being thrown a few crumbs—a hadada ibis would land heavily in the tree near the window, bouncing its weight on a thin branch, and hollering its name over and over to the iridescent starlings that pecked for their lunch on the trim lawn below. "Hadada!" it hollered, "Hadada!" It was a cry that rudely demanded attention—as if this hard-to-miss bird were afraid the world might forget its identity.

One day at lunch, a pair of best friends from India, Pooja and Sejal, sat on either side of me and leaned forward to speak in shrill, hurried whispers over me. From time to time they would include me in their banter, but they often interspersed their musical English with Hindi slang that I could not decipher, and now their stifled giggles formed an unseen barrier that I could not cross.

The door to the kitchen squeaked open, and a row of servers walked into the lunch room carrying large beige plastic trays. My belly rolled thunder, and I clutched my side, hoping no one had heard. To each table, a member of the kitchen staff in a white apron delivered a dish of overcooked mixed vegetables. The kitchen door swung open, shut, open, shut, filling the room with smells of fresh bread and oniony gravies. Then followed a basin of steamed sponge cake with a pitcher of warm vanilla custard to pour over it—something sweet to entice us to finish those limp vegetables.

We girls, with all of our varied religions and languages and nationalities and shades of ebony and copper and pink, might have formed some kind of heartwarming, we-are-the-world postcard of global peace, gathered as we were around that under-salted bowl of vegetables. Green beans and lemonade. A bloodless communion. We took and ate—Catholics, Sikhs, Hindus, Muslims, and we assorted flavors of Protestants all serving ourselves from the same dish. Warm bread arrived next in towel-lined bowls, and we ate from the same loaf. Conversation began to build, and chatter about boys and maths and field hockey filled the air: "So, which house is going to win the tournament?" "Ha! You really think he's cute?" "You got an A? You're such a swot. That exam killed me!"

Then came the platters of meat.

I looked toward the form three table across from ours and made eye contact with my friend Angela Wahome. She smiled warmly. Not long after I had arrived at this school, Angela had sought me out after a particularly grueling field hockey match (I was unused to the altitude and struggling to keep up) and had introduced herself to me. That my class was an unfamiliar crowd of teenagers claiming at least a half dozen different religions had, for the first time in my life, made my own Christian identity surprisingly uncomfortable. But Angela was a Christian. I was a Christian. To me that seemed bond enough. I smiled back.

One of the kitchen staff rounded the corner and laid a covered dish on the table. He lifted the lid, saying, simply and softly, "Pork," before moving on to the next table. The well-browned roast, sliced thick and smothered in gravy, smelled of Sunday afternoons at my grandmother's house. Comfort food. I usually gave little thought to what sort of animal had given its life for my lunch, but here in this room full of girls from practically every tribe and tongue and nation, the question could not go unanswered. We might break bread, but I could not break beef with the Hindu girls whose elbows bumped against mine. Every imaginable religious dietary restriction seemed to be represented in that room, and every restriction had to be honored. We shared a table, but we were cut off from one another by a carving knife.

I picked up the platter of steaming pork, took a slice, spooned on a little gravy, and passed it to Pooja, a Hindu, who, still giggling, took a couple slices and passed it down the table. Some girls took and some passed it on without allowing so much as a finger to touch the meat. Today it was surprisingly good—tender, well salted, and more peppery than usual. On days like this I thought of the Sikh boy in my class, a vegetarian, and pitied him for what he must not taste, must not handle, must not touch.

Minutes later, the kitchen door swung open again, and a few more servers in aprons carried new platters of meat, calling, "Beef! Beef!" A dozen or so Muslim hands shot up, and the servers worked their way along the tables, ladling cubed beef onto the plates of those with their hands in the air. Sometimes if the pork looked nasty, I'd opt for the beef along with the Muslims, but most of the time I ate the meat of the day without comment.

My Pakistani friend Shabnum sat across the table from me, eating and talking rapidly in her intensely animated way, gesturing with her fork as she spoke between bites. But when the server neared our table and again called, "Beef!" Shabnum froze. She pulled her hands back from the table and dropped her fork and knife with such a sudden recoiling, you might have thought they had transformed into a pair of serpents. She stared at her plate. She turned and stared at the server. She looked back to her plate again with wide-eyed horror. "What—." She struggled for words. "What is this? What are we eating?" Her dark eyes moved from face to face along our table, searching for reassurance.

"It's pork," Mademoiselle said bluntly.

In the bustle of the noisy lunchroom and in the excitement of sharing gossip, Shabnum had not heard the word *pork* when the server had placed the platter on the table. The meat was dark like beef, and none of the girls around her were used to paying attention to food concerns other than their own. Nobody had noticed Shabnum's mistake.

"Ohmygodohmygod. Oh my GOD!" Shabnum's chest rose in quick, shallow breaths. "Oh no. Oh God," she continued in a hoarse whisper, pushing her chair from the table with a screech against the smooth floor. She held her hand to her heart and ran out the open door and down the slope toward the hockey fields, whispering panicked curses as she went.

Mademoiselle set down her fork without a sound. The room had gone nearly silent, and she looked down the table at our bewildered faces. I could hear the sound of my own chewing, and the noise seemed strangely offensive. I stopped and held the wad of half-chewed pork inside my cheek. We had several Muslim boys in my class, but Shabnum was the only Muslim girl. None of us knew what to do. Or to say. Or even to think. We looked to our teacher whose face showed that she was clearly as uncertain as we were. At last she said softly, "Pooja. Hannah. Sejal. Go after her and see if you can cheer her up."

We glanced at each other nervously but stood. *Cheer her up? How?* Here we were, an American Presbyterian and a pair of Hindu girls, sent to bring good cheer to a young woman suffering from some kind of unspeakable turmoil of soul over a piece of roast pork. What were we supposed to do? Tell jokes? *Sooo, two Hindus and a Presbyterian walk into a bar . . . ?*

We stepped carefully down the damp grass and assessed the situation in low voices. "Did you see what happened? Was it just the pork?" "Yeah, she ate it on accident." "She thought it was beef." "That was kinda scary." "Completely. You think she's OK?" "I don't know. What do Muslims believe about doing something bad on accident?" "I have no idea." "Where did she go?"

We wandered across the lawn until we turned the corner of the pool house, where we found her in the shadows, pressing her back against the cool cinder block wall and staring at the fast-moving clouds overhead. She did not look toward us, but we could see wet streaks marking both cheeks. Her arms were folded tightly around her tall, thin body. "Shabnum?" Pooja said. No answer. "Um, I'm really sorry. Yeah. Are you OK?"

Shabnum uncrossed her arms and pressed the heels of her hands against her eyes. "No," she said.

"I'm sure it will be fine," Sejal said brightly. Shabnum did not uncover her eyes. Sejal looked at me and shrugged with a forced smile still on her face.

"Yeah," I added. "It was an accident, right? God will forgive you, if you ask Him, right?" I felt a shudder go through me. I didn't know what I was saying. *Do Muslims believe that Allah forgives? What about understandable mistakes?*

"No!" Shabnum flung her arms down. She turned her red, watering eyes toward me, and I felt my own begin to burn. "You don't understand!"

Pooja and Sejal both stepped toward her to put a hand on her shoulder. I stayed back, uncomfortable in both my skin and in my soul. The air was growing warmer, and the humidity felt like weight. Shabnum shrank away from their reach, but Pooja tried again, "Shabnum, I'm sure there are about a million people who do stuff like this—like eating the wrong thing or doing the wrong thing completely by mistake. It's not even your fault."

"I mean, it shouldn't even be a big deal," Sejal said, "'Cause you thought it was beef. Allah knows that, yeah? He knows you thought it was beef, so it wasn't, um, a sin or whatever." Sejal looked back at me and shrugged again. We were foolish girls wading into waters blacker and deeper than we could tread. My back itched, and the air grew heavier.

"Oh god!" Shabnum shouted at the grass. "You don't understand!" The three of us would-be comforters looked at each other in confusion. Shabnum glared into each of our faces and shouted again, "I might be going to hell!" That last word cracked in her throat. She slid her back down the wall, sat on the damp earth, clutched her knees, and sobbed.

A bell rang. Students from the lunch hall began to fan out across the lawn toward the various classroom buildings, and several girls looked down the hill toward us with curiosity.

"Oh god!" Shabnum wailed again, seemingly unaware of how her voice carried across the school grounds. I could not tell if she was desperately calling out to her own god or using the word *god* without thinking, but every time she said it I cringed a little.

"God won't send you to hell for eating pork by mistake!" Pooja said with a vehemence bordering on anger. It surprised me. "He wouldn't do that!"

Shabnum's tears fell on her white blouse and formed an uneven pattern of translucent dots where they landed. "You don't understand," Shabnum repeated. And she was right. I didn't.

How could I understand? I could not understand what it was to feel myself teetering on the brink of damnation. I could not understand how anyone could seek solace in a god who might, without pity, send a repentant teenage girl to hell for a cafeteria mix-up. It's true that I had no clue what Pooja's pantheon of gods might do to her if the roles were reversed and she'd accidentally bitten into a cut of beef, but her anger at Shabnum's merciless god was a feeling I *could* understand. I wanted to talk about guilt and forgiveness, about freedom from condemnation and shame, but I found no words.

Mademoiselle appeared at the top of the hill. "Time for class!" she called to us. "Are you ready?" Pooja, Sejal, and I looked at each other, unsure of whether our work here was done. What further good we could possibly do? Should we leave Shabnum alone in her misery? I shrugged. Our teacher sighed. "No? OK, ten more minutes. Then come to class."

We nodded and turned back toward Shabnum's crumpled figure. She was biting the side of her hand as she wept, and the three of us stood in silence and listened to her muffled sobs. We watched her shaking shoulders and felt the steaming air rustle our polyester skirts. "Hadada!" hollered the bird in the tree. "Hadada!" another laughed in return. "Hadada! Hadada!" The joke seemed mutual now.

"Shabnum?" I said quietly when her weeping had calmed to sniffs and sighs.

"Please go," she whispered. "Please go away. You don't understand."

In my remaining months at the school with Shabnum, we would never again speak of this incident. We would proceed as if nothing had happened, but afterward, Shabnum's friendliness seemed cooler toward me. She would still laugh, and I would laugh with her, and we would pass the plates of meat around the table as we had done before, but an invisible wedge had been driven between us. Or perhaps I had simply never noticed it before. The memory of that day would continue to trouble me for many weeks and months to come. I can only guess how it must have troubled her.

Never in all my comfortable, WASPish childhood had I encountered such crippling terror and despair, and the only words of comfort I knew how to give rested on the promises of a God that Shabnum did not know. They are still the best—and sometimes the only—words of comfort I know how to give. Watching my friend's tears fall, I might as well have been seeing her through a glass wall a thousand feet high, a thousand miles wide, and as cold as ice. I could see her, but I could do nothing to reach her. The fragile bond between us had been shattered not by war or by violence or even by angry words. It lay in ruins on account of lunch.

I turned and walked back up the hill with the two bewildered Hindu girls, and the ibis continued to laugh.

Decades after leaving Kenya, when I push my grocery cart through the checkout and see the headlines on women's magazines that say things like, "Eat What You Want—Without the Guilt!", I can picture Shabnum's thin form shuddering with fear next to the pool house at school. *That* is the kind of horror and guilt that food taboos can trigger. When it comes to the stark, painful divisions that food can create, this one childhood experience in particular stands out. It may seem out of place to talk about food fads in a book about fear, but fear of eating what is unclean is not, unfortunately, a problem confined to religious sects in distant parts of the world. Deep fear of putting the "wrong" foods into our mouths also seems to have a grip on some of the people—women in particular—within my own Christian circles and in the broader culture at large.

The preoccupation with eating the "right" foods—or the description of desserts as "sinful" or meals as "guilt-free"—troubles me. I know these descriptions might be meant as hyperbole, but words matter. These religiously charged phrases can both shape and reinforce a misguided, overblown understanding of the power food over our physical and spiritual well-being. The implication is that what we put into the body really does—contrary to Jesus' words in Matthew 15—make us unclean.

Over the years, the memory of that eighth-grade incident has returned to my mind many times when the topic of food comes up—which is often. Food is obviously a key feature of daily life, so it's no wonder we talk about it as frequently as we do. However, since moving back to the Northwest nine years ago, I've noticed that the topic of food—and its apparently countless pitfalls and temptations—seems to arise a little more often than I might wish.

WHEN MY HUSBAND AND I RETURNED TO IDAHO after our long sojourn in Texas, I had come prepared

to adjust to all the little changes that are bound to occur during a long absence, but I was surprised by just
how alien the conversations felt. I would start to catch
up with women I'd known for years, talking about a
wide variety of topics, and yet, somehow, conversation
seemed to consistently drift back toward matters of
food and health. It was almost comical how quickly a
chat at the playground would become a discussion of
turmeric tea and chlorophyll smoothies and sources of
free-range eggs.

If a person can have culture shock in her hometown, I
suppose I'd say I had it.

I am a northwest girl at heart, and I'm glad to be putting down deeper roots right here in the motherland. I've
lived in a handful of other places at various times—Iowa,
Poland, Kenya, South Africa, Texas—but the culture in
which I spent most of my growing-up years was that of
the Pacific Northwest. What that means is tough to de-
fine, but it's very much a laid-back, no-frills, full-bodied
blend that seems to draws its distinctive flavor from a
combination of Seattle grunge-and-coffee *terroir*, crisp
hints of well-chilled (and damp) left-coast beaches, the
fruity bouquet of slow-aged hippie libertinism, the bite
and astringency of a rough pioneering spirit, subtle notes
of self-righteous environmental consciousness mixed
with rifle oil, dusty overtones of collegiate intellectual-
ism, and a strong, grassy finish of no-nonsense farm life.

These are my people. It's home, and I love it. Mostly. To live among long-time friends and extended family, and to have our kids grow up in the Christian community that helped shape who I am, has been an ongoing privilege. In fact, after all the months and years of cancer treatments that Jonah endured, it's become clear that we not only love this community, we *need* it. The people here have blessed us far more than we could ever have anticipated, filling needs that we never knew we'd have. In moving back here, we were coming home to familiar faces and familiar places—to people who know our stories, both good and bad, and who both encourage and challenge us.

But I truly wasn't prepared for the prevalence of food-and-health-consciousness that seemed to have permeated the culture. Over and over again, I'd enter into conversation with other moms about familiar topics, but in a very short time, I'd feel completely at sea—or at least like I was floating down the Palouse River on a rapidly deflating inner tube.

I can't say whether all this talk of kefir grains and ancient grains was entirely new or just new to me. I did, after all, move away before I had fully entered into the mom stage of life. Before I left for Texas, other moms didn't tell me how to treat my kids' hyperactivity with elimination diets for the simple reason that I didn't have any kids old enough to get hyper in the first place. But when we returned, we came with three children in tow and one more on the way, so conversation topics naturally veered toward the care and feeding of little people.

Having kids does tend to make all of us more careful and aware of what we eat and how we look after our health. But aside from one vegan couple in their sixties, I don't remember many—if any—of my friends in the Lone Star State who tended to gravitate toward health-food-centered conversations on a regular basis in the same way that people did when we moved back to the Northwest. I suspect that the menu has since changed, but our church potlucks in Texas often involved greasy heaps of deep fried chicken, macaroni salad thick with mayo, piles of buttery biscuits, and pre-packaged, crustless PBJs for the kids. Church potlucks here, however, now involved special labeling for those adhering to a host of dietary restrictions, and the tables were now heavy on kale salads, weak on potato chips.

I don't know how much of the shift I noticed here was due to the change in my station in life and how much was due to tectonic movements in the broader culture. What I do know is that I left the Northwest under the impression that I could treat myself to a Coke once in a while without raising too many disapproving eyebrows, and I returned to a subculture where sipping a cola (particularly a *diet* cola) began to feel like an act of all-out rebellion—maybe even *sin*. I was never a great consumer of fast food and candy, but for the first time in my life, I started to worry if even my everyday food choices might make me the object of general disdain among my Christian peers. Perhaps I could cleanse my soul of my aspartame transgressions by using organic coconut oil in place of the shortening in my grandma's cookie recipe. But, on second thought, perhaps grandma's cookies still contained too much refined sugar to be counted among the truly righteous. How could I know for sure? Where could I go to learn the new food laws that now regulated our meal plans? In narrowly escaping one dietary misstep, I frequently found that I had unwittingly fallen right into another. What would people *think*?

In retrospect, I doubt anyone cared quite as deeply about these things as it first appeared, but I *felt* terribly self-conscious. What would all these mommy health experts think if they knew the truth about me and my high-fructose ways?

I had never felt self-conscious about such things before. I'd always bought groceries with far more concern for my budget than for my blood sugar. Within a couple months back in northern Idaho, however, I actually found myself fighting the impulse to strategically arrange my grocery cart so that my organic salad greens would help hide the mega-bag of generic frosted cereal underneath, lest I run into some of the ladies from church and shock them with my irresponsible food choices.

Would they actually have been shocked? Probably not. Would they have *tsk-tsk*ed silently? Maybe just a little. Was I being overly bothered by such things? Almost certainly.

Nevertheless, on this subject, I felt like the new kid in town rather than like the old-timer I believed I was. The more local ladies I added to my social media sphere, the more alarmist articles I began to see in my news feed about the unspeakable horrors of corn syrup and the dangers of GMOs. I would join old friends to chat after church and find myself confusedly trying to navigate conversations about calcium tinctures and colloidal silver supplements and spirulina powder and SCOBY babies and fish oil and lacto-fermented everything.

I had thought of myself as a reasonably well-informed woman of the world with broader-than-average tastes. But here, among my own people, I began to feel like I might need to hire a translator:

> "Can you bring me a SCOBY baby next time you come over? My mushroom died."

> "I just started putting chlorophyll in my smoothies. Have you tried that yet?"

> "You should rub a few drops of thieves on the bottom of his feet at night."

> "Are you placing another order for fermented cod liver oil gel? Cinnamon, please. I'll pay you back next week."

"I've actually been oil pulling for a month, and I really feel like it's made a difference!"

"Can you send me your recipe for lacto-fermented ketchup?"

"I'm totally going to try soaking my toenails in apple cider vinegar . . . . Yeah, I read that it can't be the cheap kind; it has to have the mother still in it."

I had never even heard the term *essential oil*—unless it meant oil that you really, really needed—until I moved back to the Northwest, and now half the people I knew seemed to smell like lavender and to be fighting colds with oil infusers and ridding their homes of hormone disrupters and dousing every bodily surface with coconut oil and purging the pantry of sugar and gluten and fermenting every locally-sourced organic thing in their crisper drawers.

Fine. I'm possibly exaggerating a little. Possibly. There's also no question that I learned quite a few helpful tips and techniques from some of these conversations. But for the first couple of years that we were back in Idaho, it truly felt as if I couldn't get through a group play date without listening to an extended discussion about some new health trend I'd never heard of, usually centered around food. Even the college students I knew were no longer binging on Mountain Dew and pizza, but were instead brewing their own kombucha, discussing where to buy raw milk, writing papers on the unintended side effects of hydrogenated fats, and even publishing their own periodicals about the dos and don'ts of food. This wasn't the Northwest I thought I remembered. I'm pretty sure it wasn't the Northwest I'd left behind.

Granted, this health-and-wellness phenomenon is not unique to the Northwest, nor has it completely taken over my sliver of the country. Most of our fast food joints are still doing pretty brisk business. We are Americans, after all, and this is still a fairly average American college town. But it does seem, at this moment, that the whole natural health movement has become far more pervasive here than it has in most other places I've been, and it took me by surprise.

The shock of moving to the fried-chicken-and-sweet-tea culture of north Texas was nothing to the shock of moving back home to find the chia-smoothie-and-quinoa culture that had apparently taken over north Idaho while I'd been away. What on earth did it all mean? And I'm not even talking about terminology. I could—and frequently did—look up words on the internet and expand my health food vocabulary easily enough. But what did it mean in terms of cultural shifts? And where did it leave me in relation to the people around me? I was almost afraid to ask.

THIS CERTAINLY WASN'T THE FIRST TIME I'D felt like a food foreigner. Visiting and living in other countries can mean culture shock of all kinds, some of which I've already mentioned, and some of which included tasting foods I never, ever thought I'd put into my mouth.

Take dairy products, for instance. I confess that I have a decades-long tendency toward dairy xenophobia. Non-American milk products? No, thanks. With the exception of European cheese, I just don't trust 'em. Pasteurized, homogenized, fortified gallon jugs for me, thanks.[25] As a teenager, I went almost entirely dairy-free the whole time my family lived overseas, partly because I feared the milk might make me sick, and partly because it just tasted funny. And the yogurt was so runny it came in bottles. Bottles, people. For drinking. If you can't stand a spoon in it, it ain't yogurt, as far as I'm concerned.

Even in the States, I couldn't avoid everything that seemed unpleasantly strange to my mainstream, American, teenage tastes. But overseas it was impossible.

Once, when my family lived in Kenya, we visited a little rural church in the middle of East Africa's Rift Valley with

25 Please, o ye well-meaning health food lobbyists, do not send me links to articles about the natural benefits of raw milk. I've probably already read them. And even if I haven't, most of my friends in this Pacific Northwest college town probably have. They can fill me in. And yes, I am already aware of the glorious balance of natural flora resident in the holistic teats of happy, grass-fed cows. Yes, Joel Salatin is a great guy. Yes, Sister Noella Marcellino is a magical cheese nun. God bless her. My mom grew up on a dairy farm, drinking raw milk from of old. She is still alive and well. My dad, however, drank one glass of the stuff and ended up in the hospital for almost a week. During college finals, no less. Natural flora with a vengeance. Call me chicken (free-range), but pasteurized cows just seem less risky.

some missionary friends. The church met inside a dung-walled hut that served as a schoolhouse during the week—with two-by-fours nailed to posts to form long, backless bench seats and shallow desks. Men sat on the right, women on the left. Our family sat all together at the back of the room—on the men's side—and I remember watching a small cockroach crawl up the sport jacket of the man directly in front of me, whose head and neck oozed with open sores.

We were invited to the pastor's home for dinner after the service, but as soon as the food was set before us, our hosts disappeared into a separate hut and left us to fig-ure out our meal by ourselves. Thankfully, our mission-ary friend explained what was on the table: chicken stew, containing all the parts—hacked into tiny fragments of meat and bone—of a whole chicken (meanwhile, live chickens were running around outside, so afflicted by parasites that most of the feathers were missing on whole patches of their backs and necks), a bowl of cold *ugali* (corn mush), *sukuma wiki* (collard greens: literally, "push [me] through the week"), and a pitcher full of a gray, gloppy beverage that resembled very wet cement.

This last item was a milk drink (horrors!) that was made by cleaning out a gourd with charcoal or ash, filling it with either cow or goat milk, burying it in the ground to keep cool, letting it sit for several days, and then dig-ging it up to serve. (I've since learned that the gourd used to make this drink is sometimes cleaned with both ash and *cow urine*, and that blood is occasionally added to the milk.) The result was essentially charcoal-fleck-ed drinkable yogurt—all natural, and full of probiotics, no doubt. In fact, it would fit so well into the current Northwest artisanal exotic food culture that some young entrepreneur in Portlandia is probably selling it to bou-tique health-food markets for $10/pint at this moment. ("Charcoalgurt®. Gray is the new white.") I ate my *suku-ma wiki*, picked at those shattered chicken parts, nibbled my *ugali*, and avoided drinking altogether.

To my palate the whole meal seemed to represent all that could possibly go wrong in the culinary world. The sad thing was that this meal most likely represented all the best that this family could afford to offer their guests, and I did not appreciate it.

These were some of the poorest people I've ever met, and they had not only fed us, but had generously given up one of their chickens to do it. Even at age thirteen, I knew that meat was not an everyday luxury for most of the world. This, for our hosts, was a feast—but that didn't make the shards of bone on my plate any less intimidat-ing. My brother made a valiant show of *mmmm*ing and nodding as he pretended to take a drink of the gray bev-erage when some of the ladies came to ask us how we were. But I went thirsty, almost to the point of dehydra-tion, rather than drink that gloppy, curdled milk flecked with black bits of burnt gourd.

If I could do it over, I think I'd give that drink a try. I think. Not so much because I'd like to know how it tastes or even to broaden my cultural horizons, but to show greater love to those selfless people who had given their best out of kindness toward us.

PART OF WHAT MAKES FOOD BOTH SO delightful and so alarming is that we need it daily, and that it comes in so many forms. We can't live without it. We're stuck in a pattern of seeking it out day after day after day. And the poorer we are, the more narrowly focused the pursuit of our daily bread must become. God made us hungry, and that hunger, as Christian scholars and theologians have observed, is ultimately a hunger for God Himself.

This persistent hunger might seem like an unfortunate limitation on our freedom, but if the foods at our disposal are in any way an accurate reflection of the God who satisfies our deepest hunger, then *infinite* and *glorious* are not far off the mark. What a shame that we have, through our fear and our scruples, pushed so much goodness off our plates. Everything from grapefruits to grasshoppers can find their way onto the menu. Creation is so packed with wildly varied foodstuffs that, from mountaintop to sea floor, the earth is basically one vast, extravagant buffet. Tables the world over are laden with creative combinations of the sweet, the savory, and the shockingly strange.

Case in point: Have you ever seen a geoduck (unfortunately pronounced "gooey-duck," as though intentionally calculated to make them even less appealing than they already are)? I will not describe their appearance lest I offend the more delicate readers, but you can *eat* those obscenely disproportioned things. One of my cousins used to be in the geoduck business, and he informed me that these fleshy shellfish sell on the Asian market for *ridiculous* sums of money. Yet not everyone—quite understandably—is inclined to serve them for supper. Especially not in polite company. We could probably divide up the whole human race between those who would happily eat geoduck and those who would not.

In fact, the *ewww* factor toward certain foods can act as a kind of shibboleth, identifying the true locals from the wannabes. Every culture has its own (often pungently fermented) edibles that tie the foreigner's stomach in knots: aged, *pieds-de-Dieu* (literally *feet-of-God*) cheeses; fire-hot vats of kimchi; nests made of cave-dwelling bird spittle; bowls of fresh baby octopuses, still waving their wee little arms as the soy sauce dribbles over their tentacles. You'll know you've finally become "one of us" when you begin to eat these things not with a grimace, but with a smile.

I get a kind of disgusted thrill over the plates of steaming horror that other people call "lunch." And I must not be alone, since there is an actual television show, now in its nineteenth season, whose entire premise is this: A guy travels around the world, eats bizarre foods, and describes the experience: "Earthy. Chewy. [Cough.] A little bit hairy." Americans have been raptly watching this food-as-extreme-sport act for nearly twenty years and don't seem to have tired of it yet.

But it's not as though the rest of the world has a monopoly on bizarre when it comes to food.

Have you ever thought about the strangeness of the all-American hot dog? When I was in high school, my family had a guest from Malawi at our Fourth of July cookout. He was shocked by the clashing, haphazard combination of toppings under which we buried our meat—ketchup, mustard, onions, tomatoes, relish. He utterly refused to try a hot dog and declared that he didn't eat meat when he couldn't tell what part of the animal it had come from. Then he added, "I'm sorry, but they're pink. They're not cooked!" We laughed and tried to convince him that they were definitely cooked, but he wouldn't believe it. So quaint.

But when my brother brought out his pet gerbil, our guest perked up and said, "Oh! In my country we eat those!" Then he explained that the men in his village would go into the grain fields at night, catch these critters, burn off their fur, dry them in the sun, then chop them into what he called relish. Here was a man who would happily turn an agricultural pest into edible rodent relish. And yet he wouldn't touch a hot dog. It kind of made me question our national taste buds.

ANY MODERATELY OBSERVANT EATER MUST have realized by now that food has a mysterious power both to unite and to divide us. There's nothing quite like mealtime to make a newcomer feel more acutely foreign. And there's nothing quite like a mealtime to make a native son feel most entirely at home—which is why I, as a longtime local, felt so disoriented by the foreignness of the eating habits I encountered in my home town.

If my recollection of Latin vocabulary serves me at all, then the *pan* in *companion* is *bread*; the mark of true companionship is, at its etymological root, the sharing of bread. In the Christian life, this clearly takes on an even deeper significance. In the breaking of bread and the giving of thanks, we commune with our God and with each other.

Food selections really can produce very noticeable fusions and fissures along cultural lines and even deeper unity and division along religious lines. I cannot forget the day my friend Shabnum wept inconsolably on the ground, fearing eternal damnation because of an accidental bite of pork.

Upon moving back to Idaho, one of the things that concerned me most about the way that food and health interests seemed to have permeated the culture here was the potential for deep fear and division that it created. I love my people, and I did fear being excluded from full fellowship by failing to toe the dietary line. Given the repeated patterns of conversation, I wondered whether my sisters in Christ might truly believe that they had a greater basis for fellowship with my backslidden Buddhist neighbor who kept his fridge stocked with free-range organics than with someone like me—with whom they broke bread at the Table of the Lord each Sunday, but who might have an occasional stash of frozen nuggets from Mega-Mart hidden in the freezer for busy weeknights.

And whenever I've dared to voice this concern, this is the point where people tend to get prickly. *Are you saying that the torture of chickens on factory farms doesn't matter to God? Are you saying that what you put in your body is irrelevant to your wellbeing? Are you telling me that food and health aren't part of a God-honoring Christian life?*

No. I'm not. At least, not exactly. What disturbs me isn't careful and conscientious eating habits *per se* so much as the high and almost paranoid priority we sometimes place on them. How we eat matters. On that we can agree. But it matters in the same way that everything we do matters to God. Jesus said that it's not what goes into the body that makes us unclean but what comes out. This principle should give us a framework for setting our day-to-day priorities.

If we're obsessed with "clean eating" but yell at our kids or mistreat our wives or lie to our employers, then no organic juice cleanse is going to wash that filth away.

If we're overcome with shame after binging on a box of Twinkies but make all kinds of allowances for the gossip and slander we pass around on social media, it's like focusing our housekeeping attention on a couple of water spots on the chrome faucet while ignoring the stinking, infectious bayou spreading across the floor around our ankles. Does this mean I am against shiny faucets? Of course not. But can we talk about the break in the sewage line for a minute before we start trying to polish the chrome?

So please don't misconstrue what I'm saying. Yes, whether we eat or drink or whatever we do, we are to do it *all* to the glory of God (1 Cor. 10:31).[26] But at the same time, Jesus specifically declares all foods to be clean (Mark 7:19, Acts 10:9–16). And, in doing so, He offended a lot of good religious people, which should give us pause.

Are we offended when a fellow Christian points out the potential spiritual pitfalls in using phrases like *clean eating* and *guilt-free food*? Are we bothered when someone

26 This passage, incidentally, concludes with some instructions to Christians *not* to bring up questions of conscience about the food set before them. There is much to chew on in this passage (ha), but is it, at the very least, *possible* that if first-century Christians weren't supposed to fret about eating beef that was sacrificed on the altar of Zeus, then perhaps twenty-first-century Christians should, similarly, worry less about whether the steak next to your mashed potatoes was sacrificed on the altar of Mammon?

raises questions about the ever-increasing number of hours and dollars that we are investing into making the "right" food choices? Are we anxiously poring over the nutrition facts on the back of every bottle in the pantry, but forgetting to drink deep from the pages of our Bibles? Do we map out, down to the exact coordinates, the geographical source of every plate of chicken, yet have only a vague idea of where our children are and no idea what they're doing at the moment? Then our priorities need to be inverted, and that right speedily.

We are sometimes in genuine danger of ignoring Christ's command to "not be anxious about your life, what you will eat or what you will drink" (Matt. 6:25a). In first-century Palestine, it's likely that the anxiety about food was predominantly about fear of going hungry or about scrupulously adhering to the Jewish food laws. But anxiety about food is still anxiety about food, and we are not at all immune to this temptation. Instead of worrying about not having enough, we now worry about eating too much. And instead of losing sleep about religiously unclean food, we fret over dietary uncleanness of a different sort.

Let me repeat: Yes, health matters. To my family, as you can imagine, it matters quite a lot. Yes, how we treat our fellow creatures—including the edible ones—matters. Yes, our care for the land and sky and seas matters. And there are, doubtless, many ways in which all of us would do well to give careful attention to these things. But our priorities matter, too. Healthful, sustainable eating, while a worthy goal in itself, frequently exerts an unhealthy precedence over matters of more eternal significance in the Christian life. Some things—many things—really should matter to us more than food. So why the constant preoccupation with what's on the menu? Isn't life more than food? Absolutely. Jesus says it is (Matt. 6:25b).

Bodily health is of real value, but its value is temporary. Spiritual health, however, is of eternal value. Good food is a wonderful way to love others, and healthy living is a wonderful way to strengthen our bodies to continue loving others for many years to come. But when our food choices form the essential boundaries of our fellowship, then mass-produced gluten loaves are not the real problem. And if our fears over clean eating prevent unity with our fellow Christians, then organic kale smoothies are not the solution. If we share the Lord's Table, then "we who are many are one body, for we all partake of the one bread" (1 Cor 10:17), and we must not let groceries become the cause of grievances among us.

To paraphrase Proverbs 17:1, better is a dry cheese puff eaten in peace than a house full of grass-fed organics with strife. Also, "Fear the Lord and depart from evil. It will be health to your flesh, and strength to your bones" (Prov. 3:7–8, NKJV). We can, I think, distill these Proverbs down to two simple conclusions: *Fear of God prevents fear of food*, and *Love trumps lunch*.

CHAPTER 16

The Clouds Ye So Much Dread

I t's always easy, living on the happy-ending side of a crisis, to talk about fear as something I've finally overcome. After all, how many heart-pounding events and terrifying expectations has God already carried me safely through? I should be pretty well catechized by now in the way God works and should know, deep in the marrow of my bones, that He's not going to abandon me the next time trouble arises. Considering all of the stories I've read and lived, I should know that, in His hands, there is truly nothing to fear.

Sometimes I do think that worry is a temptation that is behind me at last. But I can only really believe it in moments when courage isn't required of me. It's easy to feel brave when money is in the bank, health is in my bones, loved ones are by my side, the lark is on the wing, and the snail is on the thorn, so to speak. [27] But whenever a fresh uncertainty or trial confronts me, fear is always waiting there, ready to strike again and eager to sink its teeth into my soul. Every time, I must pray fervently for the strength to fight it and to trust in God's fatherly care. It's no wonder that "Fear not" is such a common refrain in the Bible; we give way to fear the way a feather gives way to wind.

That's one of the reasons that telling the stories of God's faithfulness is so valuable; these stories remind us of who He is and how He raises us up from the dust again and again. These stories also prepare us to ask for and expect this same faithfulness toward us the next time trouble comes. And it will come. The entire book of Psalms is filled with just this sort of song of deliverance: *I was afraid. Terrors surrounded me on every side. But I called out to God, and He answered me. And so I will praise Him.*

The experiences of the psalmists were not unique to them, however. Every one of us could think of stories from our own lives that shared the same themes. And even if we haven't yet lived through such terrible

27 Robert Browning, "The Year's at the Spring," quoted in *Code of the Woosters* by P.G. Wodehouse (New York: W.W. Norton & Company, Ltd., 1938), 252.

experiences ourselves, these stories of deliverance that we find in the Bible belong to all of God's people. When the Israelites annually revisited the history of their emancipation from slavery by eating the Passover lamb, they retold, generation after generation, the story of God's saving power. And in the celebrations punctuating the Christian calendar, we get to do the same: Christmas reminds us of how the Light came down and entered our darkness, and Easter reminds us of how our God has broken the chains that enslaved us to sin and death. Stories all through Scripture repeat a similar theme and should remind us again and again to *fear not.*

The reason we must be told not to fear is because fear is the understandable response to circumstances that may cause danger, suffering, or loss. It is in the very hours when fear is most natural that we are most called upon to walk by faith and not by sight.

THE STORIES OF THE MARTYRS CAN PROVIDE remarkable inspiration for Christians facing danger, trials, humiliation, torture, and even death. Think of Stephen, speaking boldly and looking to Christ while his persecutors picked up the stones that would take his life. Think of Paul and Silas, wounded by severe beatings and chained in a prison, yet still singing hymns loudly enough for the rest of the prisoners to hear. Read the Hall of Faith in Hebrews 11—the stories of those who through faith in God accomplished great things and those who, through faith in God endured "jeers and flogging, and even chains and imprisonment. They were put to death by stoning; they were sawed in two; they were killed by the sword. They went about in sheepskins and goatskins, destitute, persecuted and mistreated—the world was not worthy of them. They wandered in deserts and mountains, living in caves and in holes in the ground" (vv. 36–38, NIV).

And why are we told to think of those who have gone before us in faith? Why should we read their stories and remember their triumphs and trials? It's worth quoting the whole thing:

> Therefore, since we are surrounded by such a great cloud of witnesses, let us throw off everything that hinders and the sin that so easily entangles. And let us run with perseverance the race marked out for us, fixing our eyes on Jesus, the pioneer and perfecter of faith. For the joy set before him he endured the cross, scorning its shame, and sat down at the right hand of the throne of God. Consider him who endured such opposition from sinners, so that you will not grow weary and lose heart. (Heb. 12:1–3, NIV)

Remember the sufferings of Jesus, and remember the eternal joys to be found on the other side of the cross. Do not fear. Do not lose heart.

In the direst of circumstances, we are also called upon to cling to our God. When we pray, we are not guaranteed a change in our situation. At least not right away. That list in Hebrews 11 demonstrates that, even as we look to God in faith, some of us may face torture or even death. When Christ prayed in Gethsemane that His Father would take that awful cup from Him, the Father's answer was clearly *no* (Lk. 22:42). But that *no* was necessary for accomplishing the great work of salvation. That *no* was the means to the greatest *yes* of all. Asking with Christ that the Father's will, not ours, be done is one of the hardest requests to make when we are on the brink of something dark and dreadful. But He does not bring us through suffering for no reason. In fact, He may keep us in those circumstances for the very purpose of bringing about the good we had not yet looked for and of teaching us the wisdom that we would never have gained during our moments of ease.

Psalm 23 does not comfort us by saying, "Yea, though I walk through the valley of the shadow of death, you swoop in like Spiderman and get me the heck outta there." God does not promise to reach down and pull us out every time we ask. But He does promise to be with us. In the midst of suffering, that is our comfort; in the valley of the shadow *He is there*. He is guiding us and protecting us, like the good shepherd that He is, with His rod and staff. So I will fear no evil.

Similarly, the Psalmist doesn't say, "Thou preparest a table before me in the *absence* of my enemies." That would be nice, and sometimes He does that, too, but there is no promise here that these enemies will be immediately scattered. Of course, in the end, we know that God will make all of His enemies a footstool under the feet of Christ (Ps. 110:1). But in Psalm 23, the enemies remain. And yet, He pours out His blessings—to the point of overflowing—right there, in the middle of enemies all around. We do not—must not—wait for circumstances to change before we cast aside our fear. Darkness may surround us on every side, but if the Light of the World is with us, what can the darkness do? If God is for us, who can be against us (Rom. 8:31)?

I SUSPECT THAT MANY CHRISTIANS—ESPECIALLY the older ones—could tell you that some of the most harrowing moments in their lives were the ones that most powerfully revealed the mercy and love of God. As I've already shown, that's been the case for me. The greatest dangers, and the things I dreaded most, were the very things that have served to show me that I can trust God, at all times, to work everything for good (Rom. 8:28)—and not just for my good personally, but very often for the good of those standing by, seeing those events unfold. When we Christians affirm God's goodness in our suffering, when we speak of our enduring hope in the midst of grief, when we demonstrate deep peace as we lie on our death beds, and when we count it joy as we encounter various trials, it works for the good of all the rest of us who witness it. Remaining steadfast in our faith at the times when fear would be most natural helps to bolster the courage of other believers and deepens their trust in the Father who cares for His beloved children.

This, again, is why we need these stories. The stories of Scripture and the stories of God's people who have gone before us should shape our hearts and minds and should show us how to read the events of our own lives—and to trust the Author. That is the point of this book.

In the absence of these stories, fear can gain a much more powerful foothold. We rich, complacent Christians with our safe, cushy lives, are not accustomed to the kinds of trials that would *daily* turn us to a conscious reliance on God. We are the self-made men. We're out of practice when it comes to seeking God's blessings because we're already overflowing with blessings that we don't readily acknowledge as blessings at all; we think of them as rights, and we resent any God that might take them from us. We don't anchor ourselves with deep theological truth while times are good, and so we are tossed with the wind whenever storm clouds roll in. We don't look *back* on the good that God has already accomplished through suffering—both in our lives and in the lives of others—and so we don't know how to look forward to it, either.

Scripture is food, but we're like picky toddlers who refuse to eat anything but the French-fry-and-sugar-cube verses. We spit out the meat of theology and consume the junk food of bumper-sticker platitudes—and then we expect it to get us through the marathon of life. We are blissfully unaware of how spiritually flabby and out of shape we are. In fact, we're pretty impressed with the sensation of the wind in our hair as we go coasting along the downhill stretches of life with our Jesus fish decals bearing witness to our spiritual strength. Life is good, and we are just so (hashtag)blessed!

But when we come up against the steep and imposing hills (cancer, death, betrayal), we are shocked to find how quickly we lose both our breath and the will to go on. *Hey!* We think. *This is haaard! Looks like God isn't so good after all.*

God is, of course, merciful. Many are the times when I've cried out to God, feeling that I can't go another inch, and He has pushed me along in spite of my failures. But it's not uncommon for Christians to collapse and give up, looking at themselves and then at the steep road ahead, and refusing to listen to His promises. How many—how *many!*—professing Christians have abandoned the faith after some deeply painful event in their lives? Why? Did they think that God would never let anything painful happen to His children? If so they don't really know who He is. Have they considered Job? Do they know about

David running for his life in the wilderness? Have they read of Joseph, sold into slavery and languishing in the Egyptian prison? Have they meditated on the plight of Mary? Do they know the story of Jesus at *all*?

We need these stories—and the truths that accompany them—to fill our souls and strengthen us for the battles ahead. If we are steeped in the knowledge of God's goodness, we will not be so easily offended when well-meaning friends bring it to mind in the midst of our pain. To a soul that clings to God's faithfulness during the good times, the words *all things for good* should strike us during the bad times not as an empty cliché or a thoughtless offense, but as an eternal comfort.

We can also reinforce our convictions that God is good by gratefully acknowledging the ways that He has turned evil on its head in our own lives. Lots of people like to quote Philippians 4:7–8 when faced with fearful trials, but the phrase "with thanksgiving" is often overlooked. Gratitude for God's past and promised mercies is an important part of what He uses to usher in the peace that passes understanding: "Do not be anxious about anything, but in everything by prayer and supplication *with thanksgiving* let your requests be made known to God. And the peace of God, which surpasses all understanding, will guard your hearts and your minds in Christ Jesus." To be grateful—even for the "fleas" in our lives—requires taking the time to recognize the goodness bestowed upon us by a good God, which is why gratitude serves as daily training for the battle against fear. So recognize the goodness of God. And then thank Him.

What danger or trial or sorrow has He brought you through and used to teach you wisdom or bring you joy? Can you finally say, like Joseph to his treacherous brothers, "You meant evil against me, but God meant it for good" (Gen. 50:20)? These stories do not happen just in the pages of the Bible; they happen in our lives, too.

In a culture of gushy, Instagrammy, Christian-ishness, "God is good" can usually be translated as "God gave me a new car," or "I got a better job," or "Wedding day!" or "Date night," "Cute kids," "Beach vacation," and so on. Life is picturesque and easy, so yeah, God is good.

But is God still good when you get fired, drive a junker, are betrayed by a friend, lose your loved one, or learn that your kid has cancer? What is God then? Is He good? And what are you? Are you still *#blessed*?

It's easy to say He's good when hard things are happening to other people. But are we singing the same tune when the hard thing happens to us? Do we *really* believe that God is good? Or do we actually believe that God is nothing but a fickle tyrant—one we must flatter with glowing sentiments when we're sitting in the lap of luxury, and on whom we can simply turn our backs when we're sitting in the ashes of sorrow? Dear Christian, would you turn away from the God you say is good if anything truly painful were to happen to you? Then the God you believe in *isn't* the one you pretend to worship.

CLEARLY, OUR FATHER DID NOT INTEND FOR me—or any of us—to stay cocooned in our little comfort zones forever. Looking ahead to the future, I usually wish He did want us there. But looking back, I am so very grateful that He doesn't. I don't want to go through any more trials. But I can't be anything but thankful for what He has already given me and taught me through the trials that are now behind me.

I don't doubt that the years ahead will bring new dangers and fresh sorrows, but as I look back in gratitude, I can also look forward in faith and know that God is with me and that He is up to something better than what I can see before my face in the moment. For our good, He intends for us to grow, even when the growing pains may be excruciating. We can endure hardship because we know that God is treating us as His own children (Heb. 12:7).

My five boys love to hear about our family history, but the stories they love most are the ones that involve some sort of danger or crisis. These stories almost always resolve with a greater joy or deeper wisdom than could be found in moments of ease and comfort. These are the stories I love best, as well. And I think we love them for much more than their entertainment value; we love them because they teach us how to rightly understand our own place in the story of the world—a world that is filled at once with beauty and with brokenness, with glory and with grief. Through these harrowing bits of history, we can more clearly see where we've come from, who we are now, who God is, and where this grand narrative is going.

God wants His children to remember and recount the biggest stories of mercy and deliverance; He put them into a book for us and included just enough spoilers to give away the happy ending to all of history. (Hint: There will be a wedding.) And as imitators of God, we can remind our own children of the joy that is coming and of the unique stories of deliverance in our lives. Some of mine are in this book. I want my children to remember how good God has been to me—and to all of us. The darker the storm cloud, the more drenched we have been by the downpour of mercy. So we as Sarah's children need not fear anything that is frightening.

> Ye fearful saints, fresh courage take,
> The clouds ye so much dread
> Are big with mercy, and shall break
> In blessings on your head.
>
> —William Cowper[28]

---

28 William Cowper, "Light Shining out of Darkness" in *The Poems of William Cowper, Esq.* (London: J. Limbird, 1824), 410.

61967700R00139

Made in the USA
Middletown, DE
16 January 2018